**Books are to be returned on or before
the last date below.**

3|19.

LIBREX —

A Cost Too Far?

An analysis of the net economic costs & benefits
for the UK of EU membership

Ian Milne

With a foreword by
the Rt Hon Lord Weatherill,
Speaker of the House of Commons 1983-1992

Civitas: Institute for the Study of Civil Society
London

First published July 2004
Second edition August 2004

© The Institute for the Study of Civil Society 2004
77 Great Peter Street
London SW1P 2EZ
Civitas is a registered charity (no. 1085494)
and a company limited by guarantee, registered in
England and Wales (no. 04023541)

email: books@civitas.org.uk

ISBN 1-903 386-37 3

Typeset by Civitas
in Times New Roman 11pt

Printed in Great Britain by
The Cromwell Press
Trowbridge, Wiltshire

Contents

Author

Ian Milne has been the Director of the cross-party think-tank Global Britain since 1999. He was the founder-editor (in 1993) of *The European Journal*, and the co-founder (in 1995) and first editor of *eurofacts*. He is the translator of *Europe's Road to War*, by Paul-Marie Coûteaux, and the author of numerous pamphlets, articles and book reviews, mainly about the relationship between the UK and the European Union.

He is chairman of companies involved in manufacturing, publishing and book distribution. He has degrees in engineering and business administration, and a forty-year career in industry and merchant banking in the UK, France and Belgium.

Second Edition

The text is mostly unaltered, but we have taken the opportunity presented by demand for a reprint of 5,000 copies to respond to comments by some early reviewers.

Foreword

'Let the battle be joined', said the Prime Minister when he announced that we are to be allowed a referendum on the new EU Constitution. He is to be congratulated. For far too long all our main political parties have denied the British people a full and open debate about their growing relationship with the EU.

When I entered Parliament as the Member for Croydon North East, in 1964, I had campaigned on the slogan 'Truth in Politics'. Since then there has been a steady erosion of trust by the electorate in the truth of what they are told by politicians.

At the time of our entry into what was then the European Common Market, in 1972, I was the Conservative Government's Deputy Chief Whip. I supported entry on the assurance of the Prime Minister, Mr Edward Heath, that 'joining the Community does not entail a loss of national identity or an erosion of essential national sovereignty'.

It would be wrong of me now, as a former Speaker of the House of Commons, to comment on the conclusions of this short study. The author, Ian Milne, finds that our present membership of the EU is very expensive in economic terms, amounting to perhaps four per cent of our Gross Domestic Product annually. He uses official figures to support his case.

Mr Milne does not venture into the broader question as to whether our membership of the EU is helpful or unhelpful to our democracy, to the right of the British people to govern themselves, to elect and dismiss those who make their laws. I trust that national debate will also develop on these important matters as well as on the economic advantages or disadvantages.

As a former Speaker, however, I do know that Parliamentarians now have a sacred duty honestly to explain the pros and cons of our developing relationship with the European Union. Only then can the people make an informed choice.

In Parliament the Prime Minister has rightly said, 'It is time to dispel the myths about Europe.' A debate is urgently needed and this penetrating study is a good place to start. So to echo the Prime Minister—let the battle commence.

The Rt Hon Lord Weatherill
Speaker of the House of Commons, 1983 – 1992

Editor's Introduction

What would be the economic consequences of leaving the EU? Prime Minister Blair often claims that 60 per cent of the UK's trade and three million jobs 'depend on' our EU membership. Closer analysis reveals this to be a highly misleading claim.

Sixty Per Cent of Our Trade? The first problem with Mr Blair's statement is that it refers to 'goods' and not 'goods and services'. In 2002, 59 per cent of UK exports of 'goods' were exported to the other 14 EU countries.[1] However, it is more usual to count exports of both 'goods and services' and, in 2002, UK exports of goods and services to the EU comprised about 52 per cent of the UK total. As the author of the current study has shown, this figure needs to be adjusted for the Rotterdam-Antwerp distortion. These two huge ports serve as transit points for goods on their way to other parts of the world, but the official figures assume that goods sent there are going to the EU. After adjustment, 48 per cent of UK exports of goods and services go to the EU.

Sixty Per Cent of Our Economy? The second misconception is that 60 per cent of our *economy* depends on the EU, whereas the true figure is more like ten per cent. Exports of goods and services only account for 21 per cent of 'final demand'.[2] If exports of goods and services to the EU account for 48 per cent of total exports, then ten per cent of GDP is currently the result of exports of goods and services to other EU members.[3] In other words, 79 per cent of our economy is the result of domestic activity, involving buying from and selling to each other, and exports of goods and services to the rest of the world account for 11 per cent.

Three Million Jobs Would Go? Mr Blair's third mistake is to believe that the jobs currently resulting from trade with the EU would be lost if we left. However, a number of authoritative studies have found that leaving the EU would have little impact on jobs, including a report by the National Institute for Economic and Social Research,[4] and a report for the US Congress by the US International Trade Commission.[5] In particular, if the UK left the EU, it is unlikely that UK companies would be denied access to other EU markets. The latest figures are for the period before enlargement and show that the other 14 members exported more to the UK than they imported from us.[6] It might be said that they need the UK more than the UK needs them. Moreover, now that 20 countries from Switzerland to Egypt have free trade agreements with the EU, it would be extraordinary if the UK could not negotiate a similar deal. In trading relations, self-interest tends to prevail, but in any event the EU's average external tariff on non-EU imports is down to about 1.5 per cent[7] and the World Trade Organisation would prevent any 'retaliation', however improbable.

Would there be a cost of leaving the EU?

The author concludes that, if the UK were to leave the EU, there would be no net loss of jobs or trade. However, to draw any such conclusion involves complex calculations, and it is widely accepted that assumptions have to be made that can influence the final figure. The author provides a range of estimates from 'rock bottom', through 'most likely', to 'high'. His rock-bottom figure draws largely on official sources and deploys the most cautious of assumptions. The net costs of EU membership are appraised in five areas: EU regulation, the common agricultural policy, net payments to EU institutions, the single market, and inward investment. In keeping with earlier cost-benefit studies the author's results are expressed as a percentage of GDP. In this Introduction the estimates are in pounds. Overall, the net cost of remaining in the EU ranges from the rock-bottom estimate of £15 billion to the 'most likely' of £40 billion.

EU Regulation: The rock-bottom estimate is £5 billion (rounded down from £6 billion) and the most likely, £20 billion. Based on the Government's own regulatory impact assessments (RIAs), the total cost of regulation between 1999 and 2004 (one-off costs spread over the period plus recurring costs), according to the British Chambers of Commerce, was £7.91 billion per year.[8] Based on information supplied by the House of Commons Library in May 2004, 83 per cent of the cost of regulations originated in EU directives. If rounded down to 80 per cent, then about £6.33 billion of the £7.91 billion total cost is due to the EU. There were no RIAs before 1999 and the estimate for the period from 1973 to 1999 has to be more tentative. An official study of the overall impact of EU regulation in the Netherlands has put the figure at two per cent of GDP.[9] If also true of the UK, the net cost would be £20 billion.

CAP: The rock-bottom figure is £5 billion (after rounding down from £7 billion) and the most likely, £15 billion. An OECD study put the total cost to the EU in 2002 at 1.4 per cent of GDP (the UK figure today would be £14 billion).[10] Allowing for costs and subsidies not included in the OECD study, and for subsidies received by UK farmers, the most likely figure is £15 billion.

Payments to EU Institutions: This is an annual figure published by the Office for National Statistics and so no range is given. The latest *Pink Book* shows net payments of £4.3 billion. Over the last ten years, the UK has paid a similar net average amount each year, paying out an average of £11 billion per annum and receiving back £7 billion in 'aid'.[11]

Single Market: A study by the European Commission in 1996 and an academic study published in 1998 are often quoted in support of the claim that the single market raised total EU output by between one and 1.5 per cent.[12] However, a number of independent studies have found no hard evidence of net benefits. For example, the Bundesbank could find no evidence that it has helped German trade.[13] The UK economy is unlikely to be any different. The Institute of Directors reviewed studies from the Commission, the OECD and others and noted the absence of persuasive evidence of the benefits of the single market.[14] In 2003 an Institute of Directors' survey of members found that trading in the EU-14 was on balance unattractive and more costly, with more paperwork than before the single market. The overall conclusion is that the balance of costs and benefits for the UK economy is zero, that it could be negative, and that the UK would not suffer economically by being outside the single market.

Inward Investment: The UK is one of the world's leading overseas investors, but also a recipient of significant inward foreign direct investment (FDI). UK Trade and Investment, part of the DTI, monitors investment flows and its annual review for 2002/03 lists the main reasons why the UK attracts investment. Access to the single market is one among several other advantages, including the skilled and English-speaking labour force, the flexible labour market, good communications, the strong science and technology base in universities, low corporation tax, ease of market entry and tax allowances for start-ups.[15] These other advantages would remain and, if the UK left the EU, the impact on inward investment is likely to be neutral.

Some studies, including one by the NIESR, claim that FDI would fall if the UK left the EU.[16] The author questions this contention by looking at the earnings on all inward investment made by the main economic sectors. The two biggest are oil and gas (39 per cent of earnings) and financial services (18 per cent). He argues that oil and gas would continue to attract investment because they are high value products in a stable part of the world. Investments in financial services, another global industry, are mainly denominated in US dollars, and will go wherever the best return is to be found. The City has not suffered from the introduction of the euro and would be unlikely to suffer if the UK left the EU. The author accepts that investment in manufacturing of 'chemicals, plastics and fuel products' (10 per cent by earnings) and 'other industries' (11 per cent) might be influenced by our EU membership, but argues that it is a factor of declining importance.

Hitched to a 'Falling Star'?: The author questions whether it is wise to link our fortunes to a region of the world with a poor record of economic growth and whose share of both world markets and GDP is destined to fall. Even the European Commission takes a gloomy view of the EU's prospects.[17] In its December 2002 review it forecast a 44 per cent decline in the EU-15 share of global GDP from 18 per cent in 2000 to ten per cent in 2050. In 2050, as in 1950 and 2000, the three most populous countries in the world are likely to be India (1.6 billion), China (1.5 billion) and the USA (0.4 billion). The working-age population of the EU, even after its current enlargement to 25 members, is projected to decline by 20 per cent to 30 per cent by 2050; whereas the working-age population of the USA is expected to increase by nearly one-third.

Civitas does not take a corporate view about leaving the EU, but a calm and measured public debate is long overdue and Ian Milne's essay is an admirable effort to illuminate the discussion.

David G. Green

Preface

The European Union is a political project. It is not about economics, though its economic consequences are profound.

British participation in *le projet européen,* and whether that participation should continue, and in what form, is thus primarily a question of politics. But the politics cannot be assessed without an understanding of the economics. This paper, like others before it, aims to evaluate the economic costs and benefits of UK membership of the EU.

Any cost-benefit analysis of EU membership is necessarily a complex business. That is no excuse for not doing the exercise. Most great projects, in politics, in war, in business—indeed, in life generally—involve weighing-up complex alternative courses of action with attendant risks, threats and opportunities. In 2003 HM Treasury carried out an immensely complex cost-benefit analysis of whether the UK should participate in an undertaking fundamental to the European project: the euro. In the course of its study HM Treasury—as it had to—made economic, demographic and political judgements about the future, often on the basis of incomplete information. It concluded that the costs outweighed the benefits.

HM Government was right to assess the economic costs and benefits of adopting the euro. The case for a comprehensive fully-resourced cost-benefit analysis of UK participation in the European project itself—the European Union—is even stronger.

The exercise which follows, modestly-resourced, does not claim to be the definitive answer to the question: are we economically better off in or out of the EU? It should be considered rather as a feasibility study for the comprehensive exercise which, as decision time approaches on the European Constitution, is urgently needed.

Ian Milne
London, June 2004

Notes on Sources

The British and US Governments, the UK's Office for National Statistics, the International Monetary Fund, the World Bank, the World Trade Organisation, the United Nations, the Organisation for Economic Cooperation and Development, Eurostat, the European Commission and the Bundesbank are the prime data sources.

Chapter 2 is based on the British Government's own cost-benefit analyses of legislative acts ('Regulatory Impact Assessments').

Many of the detailed studies on which this paper is based have been published as Global Britain Briefing Notes, and can be found at www.globalbritain.org

Summary

- The balance of the costs and benefits of UK membership of the EU is unequivocally negative. The net costs are substantial

- The current recurring annual direct net cost to the UK of EU membership is estimated to range between approximately three and five per cent of GDP, with a 'most likely' figure of four per cent of GDP, equivalent to £40 billion per year

- To illustrate the magnitude of that amount, the UK defence budget is £27 billion a year, while excise duties (on drink, fuel and tobacco) raise £40 billion a year

- Within the 'most likely' £40 billion, £20 billion is the direct net cost of EU regulation to the UK economy—annually

- A further £15 billion is the direct net cost to the UK economy of the Common Agricultural Policy

- Another £4.3 billion is the annual cash subsidy that the UK pays to 'Brussels' through the EU Budget

- The current heavy burden of direct net economic cost—four per cent of GDP—will not get lighter in future. At best it will get no worse

- The more likely scenario is for the current heavy burden of net economic cost to worsen—perhaps dramatically

- The gloomy prognosis for the future is due partly to measures already in the EU pipeline, starting with the EU Constitution and enlargement, and partly to the UK being locked in to a regional bloc in marked long-term decline

- Opportunity cost—growth foregone through not being able to pursue opportunities outside the EU—could make the total net cost of EU membership even higher

- On a global view, the EU model of conducting trade, via a tightly-regulated customs union, is outmoded. The world outside the EU, with a superior trading and economic performance, tends to choose interlocking networks of user-friendly free trade agreements. These deliver the same benefits that EU members derive from the Single Market, but with very few of the costs

- None of four recent authoritative cost-benefit analyses, nor a fifth one in progress, includes opportunity costs, and none concludes that EU membership delivers a significant net economic benefit to the UK

- Two of the five cost-benefit analyses cited above conclude—like this paper—that the net cost to the UK of EU membership is substantial

- The assumptions used throughout this paper are carefully spelt out, and believed to be unexceptional.

1

Cost versus Benefit—the Calculus

Eight basic economic facts about the UK-EU relationship are listed to set the context in which estimates are made. Direct costs and benefits are assessed for each of five main categories (not including the Common Fisheries Policy or the effect of the UK's structural trade deficit with the EU). Estimates are expressed to the nearest half-percentage point of UK GDP, and rated according to reliability.

The outcome is a 'most likely' total current net direct cost of four per cent of GDP per year, within a range stretching from a 'rock-bottom' low of 1.5 per cent GDP to a high of over five per cent. Net cost is unlikely to diminish in future as seven measures already in the EU pipeline come into effect.

1. The context

At the forefront of any realistic assessment of the economic costs and benefits of UK membership of the EU are eight overwhelming basic facts, often forgotten in discussion about the UK and the EU—'elephants in the room', so big they aren't noticed:

- The proportion of the British economy—and the proportion of British jobs—involved in exporting to EU-14 is about ten per cent (see Figure 1.1 p. 2 and Appendix II, p. 60).

- Nevertheless, the UK has to impose the totality of the EU *acquis communautaire* on the 90 per cent of the economy which is **not** involved in exporting to EU-14

- The benefits of free trade with the EU's Single Market are available to countries outside the EU through bilateral agreements such as the EU-Mexico Free Trade Agreement,[1] with few if any of the legislative and other costs of membership of the Single Market

- Well under half—around 45 per cent—of all British exports (goods, services, income, transfers) go to EU-14 (see Appendix II: Table A2.1, p. 60)

- EU-14 is in structural surplus on its trade with its single biggest customer, the UK(see chapter 6)

- The UK is the third biggest exporting nation[2] and the fourth biggest economy[3] in the world

- Barriers to global trade (both tariff and non-tariff), especially between OECD countries, are already very low (two per cent or less) and tending to zero (see chapter 10.3, p. 45)

- In the case of the UK, 92 per cent by value of all its imports are tariff-free (see chapter 10.3, p. 45).

Figure 1.1
The Proportion of the UK Economy
Involved in Exporting to the EU-14

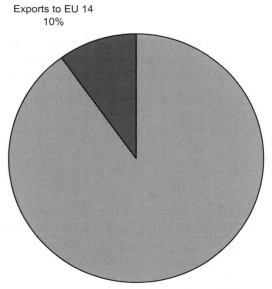

Exports to EU 14
10%

Domestic Economy &
Exports to Rest of World
90%

2. *Methodology*

The current direct costs and benefits of EU membership are assessed by category, separately, under the following five headings:

- Regulation
- Common Agricultural Policy (CAP)
- EU Budget
- Single Market
- Inward Investment

These categories are not the only ones by which the economic costs and benefits of EU membership can be measured; but they include the main headings considered by previous cost-benefit analyses, and the topics which appear to dominate debate about the economic relationship between the UK and the EU.

One category not considered here (because of insufficiently robust data) where costs may significantly exceed benefits is the Common Fisheries Policy (CFP).

Detailed calculations by category are set out in Chapters 2 to 6. Where appropriate, an overall range of possible net direct costs or benefits is given, and, within that range, the author's best guess at a plausible 'most likely' point. The total figure for the *current* most likely net direct economic cost/benefit of EU membership is set out below in Table 1.1.

Chapter 7 asks how the UK would have done, economically, had it not been in the EU. It suggests various approaches to establishing opportunity cost and comes up with an estimate derived from a comparison of the performances of the UK and of a peer group of countries with which the UK has strong affinities.

Chapter 8 looks at scenarios for the future.

In a limited exercise of this kind it would be misleading to aim for spurious precision. The best that can be done is to estimate broad magnitudes. Those calculated here are expressed to an 'accuracy' of one half of one per cent of GDP, which at present UK values (see Appendix VI) is equivalent to £5 billion per year. (Several previous cost-benefit exercises adopted similar approaches.)

The reliability or robustness of the underlying statistical data, and the explicit and implicit assumptions involved in processing it, are classified according to a rating system with four levels: AA (very high); A (high); B (medium); C (low). Though not in any way scientific it is hoped the reader will accept them as being devised in good faith as a guide to comprehension.

3. The most likely current net cost

The result, set out below, is a 'most likely' annual direct net cost of four per cent of GDP, equivalent to £40 billion at current levels of UK GDP:

Table 1.1
***'Most likely' current direct net economic costs
and benefits of EU membership***

Chapter	Page no.	Category	Cost	Benefit	Annual net cost as proportion of GDP (%)	Reliability of estimate
2	6	Regulation	Yes	Yes	2	B
3	10	CAP	Yes	Yes	1.5	A
4	13	EU Budget	Yes	Yes	0.5	AA
5	16	Single Market	Yes	Yes	zero	A
6	19	Inward Investment	No	No	zero	A
		Total			4	

Please note that the economic impact of EU membership on UK jobs is implicit in the calculations for the Single Market and Inward Investment; it is not considered separately. Some recent cost-benefit analyses (see Chapter 9) explicitly considered the impact on UK jobs of withdrawal from the EU.

4. Direct net cost: the range of estimates

The detailed, 'bottom-up' assumptions and calculations are set out in Chapters 2 to 6. The assumptions are believed to be unexceptional, modest and realistic, even at the upper end of the range. Readers will make up their own minds whether they agree. It can be seen in Table 1.2 below (Cols 2, 3 and 4) that, expressed as percentages of GDP, the outcome is substantial.

As a further test of the plausibility of the range, minimalist, 'rock-bottom' estimates have been made (Col 1), essentially in respect of EU Regulation and of the CAP. The EU Budget rock-bottom direct net cost is the bare cash balance between UK payments to and receipts from EU Institutions, not an estimate: a rounded-up half of one per cent of GDP. The rock-bottom estimates sum to 1.5 per cent of GDP, equivalent to £15 billion a year. The fact that, even with minimalist (not to say highly implausible) assumptions, the total net cost estimate comes out at that level, may be taken as an indication that the estimates made with unexceptional assumptions in Cols 2, 3 and 4 are only too plausible.

Table 1.2
**Range of Estimates of Current Direct Net Cost
in Percentages of GDP**

Category	Col. 1: Rock-bottom estimate	Unexceptional Assumptions		
		Col. 2: Lower end of range	Col. 3: Most likely	Col. 4: Upper end of range
Regulation	0.5	1	2	3
CAP	0.5	1.2	1.5	1.7
EU Budget	0.5	0.5	0.5	0.5+
Single Market	zero	zero	zero	more than zero
Inward Investment	zero	zero	zero	zero
Totals	**1.5**	**2.7**	**4**	**5.2+**

5. Calculation: the future

Chapter 8 considers seven future measures, already in the pipeline, starting with the EU Constitution and Enlargement, which could have an impact in the years to come on the net cost for the UK of membership of the EU. In each case, compared to the existing net cost set out above, the likely scenario is for an additional net cost for the UK. The cumulative increase in net cost potentially arising from these pipeline measures is deliberately not quantified. However, it seems reasonable to suppose that the additional future net direct cost could be significant—that is to say, counted in multiples of one per cent of UK GDP annually, perhaps in double figures.

2

The Cost of EU Regulation

Net cost or benefit for the UK economy?

Over half of UK legislation is EU-initiated. An analysis of government Regulatory Impact Assessments allows quantification of some, but by no means all, of the costs, but not the benefits, of EU legislation. Dutch research, and UK survey evidence, looks to be consistent with the RIA-derived estimates.

Scoreboard

Net Cost or Benefit	Net Cost
Most Likely Net Cost	Two per cent of GDP
Range of Estimates	One to three per cent of GDP
Reliability of Estimate	B

The British government admits that 'about half of major UK laws start off in Europe'.[1] In addition, since 1973, it has enacted directly in the UK a minimum (it does not know the precise number) of 101,811 EU regulations.[2] Clearly, the impact of EU legislation in the UK is on its way to fulfilling the prediction made over a decade ago by Jacques Delors, that 80 per cent of member states' laws would soon be made in Brussels.

BCC Burdens Barometer

An indication of what is almost certainly the minimum regulatory cost to UK business of both UK and EU initiated legislation comes from the 'Burdens Barometer' compiled by the British Chambers of Commerce (BCC).[3] This is the only systematic and objective attempt at quantifying regulatory costs in the UK. It is based on an ongoing analysis, carried out jointly by London and Manchester

Business Schools, of the government's own Regulatory Impact Assessments (RIAs), which began in 1999. Not all RIAs contain monetary cost and benefit estimates of the consequences of implementing the legislation concerned, and none contains estimates of the knock-on and induced costs. The Burdens Barometer tabulates costs (quantified in around 70 per cent of RIAs) but is unable to provide estimates of benefits since only 20 per cent of RIAs quantify benefits (and only seven per cent quantify 'benefits for consumers'). Although the BCC believe that coverage of UK-originated RIAs is complete, 'the picture is less clear for the EU-originated legislation'.

Over the five-and-a-half years 1999 to mid-2004, the government's own RIAs estimate the one-off costs of the new legislation concerned (excluding the cost of the National Minimum Wage) at £5.13 billion, an average of £0.93 billion per year over those five-and-a-half-years. In addition, the recurring cost of new legislation is estimated at £6.98 billion per year, making a total (one-off costs spread over the period plus recurring costs) of £7.91 billion per year. Approximately 80 per cent by value of that cost appears to be EU-initiated,[4] so the EU-related cost would be 80 per cent of £7.91 billion or £6.33 billion. The key legislative acts concerned followed the UK's acceptance of the Social Chapter in 1997.

What about EC/EU legislation implemented in the UK prior to that: on accession in 1973 and in the 26 years from 1973 to 1998? Neither RIAs nor any other estimates appear to exist for the pre-1998 period, so a broad assumption has to be made. If it is assumed—very conservatively—that such legislation imposed a regulatory burden equivalent to that imposed between 1999 and 2004, of £6.33 billion per year (in other words at an average rate of cost imposition over those 26 years about five times *lower* per year than between 1999 and 2004) the total recurring cost of all EC/EU-initiated legislation enacted between 1973 and 2004 works out at present at £12.66 bn per year. If it is assumed further—an unexceptional assumption, for the reasons set out below in Chapter 8 (p. 32)—that EU legislation will continue to be implemented in the next five-and-a-half years at the same rate as in the last five-and-a-half, the total regulatory cost would rise to £18.99 billion per year by 2009—equivalent to two per cent of GDP at present GDP levels.

That figure is for the cost side of the equation only. What might the benefits be? Some EU legislation presumably has benefits for the UK, even if government RIAs seem strangely coy about quantifying them. On the other hand, the Burdens Barometer only covers 70 per cent of all RIAs produced, and coverage of EU legislation—where 80 per cent of the cost seems to be—is patchy. Not all EU Directives are covered by RIAs, while the far more numerous EU Regulations—which are automatically binding in member states without national parliamentary approval—are not covered at all. RIAs, moreover, assess direct costs only, and take no account of the knock-on and induced impact of regulation. Setting the putative benefits arising from EU legislation against the costs that the Burdens Barometer does not capture, it is safe to assume that for the UK economy the *current* overall regulatory cost of EU legislation, net of benefit, is closer to two per cent of GDP than one per cent.

Dutch experience is similar

The Dutch Vice Prime Minister and Finance Minister, Mr Gerrit Zalm, estimated recently[5] that in his country the administrative burden for business was four per cent of GDP, and that 'over 50 per cent' had a 'direct European origin'—implying that the EU-related administrative burden on Dutch business is over two per cent of GDP. Given the well-known British propensity to 'gold-plate' EU legislation, the UK percentage is likely to be higher.

Evidence from UK business surveys

How do businesses perceive the regulatory burden? In 2003 an IoD members' survey[6] found that trading in the EU-14 was on balance unattractive and, moreover, more costly, with more paperwork, than pre-Single Market, suggesting that the costs of the Single Market outweighed its benefits. Even the pro-EU *Single Market News*, polling its readership for its 'Internal Market Scoreboard' in 2002, could find only 26 per cent of respondents who thought that the impact of the internal market had been positive—admittedly more than the 17 per cent who thought it had been negative, but not exactly a ringing endorsement. Though directed at UK exporters rather than at UK business as a whole, such survey evidence suggests that the burden of EU legislation/regulation is significant at the very least, and that the costs outweigh the benefits.

Rock-bottom estimate

An absolutely minimal 'rock-bottom' net cost of EU regulation can be estimated by counting only the direct RIA-derived net cost—about £6 billion a year—arising from the implementation in the UK of EU Directives over a very short period, the five-and-a -half years 1999 to mid-2004. Excluded from this estimate are costs arising from the imposition in the UK of the totality of the 1973-1998 *acquis communautaire*, consisting of EU Directives, EU Regulations and case law. Rounded to the nearest half-percentage point of GDP, this gives a rock-bottom estimate of one half of one per cent.

Conclusion

Net of benefits that some EU legislation brings for UK business and consumers, the figures derived from the BCC data suggest a net cost of EU regulation for UK business of close to two per cent of GDP—coincidentally about where Mr Zalm comes out in respect of the Netherlands. Given the big assumptions that have to made, especially about the impact of EU legislation in the UK for the 26 years prior to 1999, the possible range is put at between one and three per cent of GDP—but it could be much higher.

3

The Common Agricultural Policy (CAP)

Net cost or benefit for the UK economy?

In EU-15's deliberations on the CAP British interests are largely ignored: the UK share of EU-15 farm output is low and continental farm lobbies are powerful. The CAP playing field is thus strongly tilted against the UK, resulting in a heavy preponderance of cost over benefit, with UK taxpayers paying subsidies to other EU farmers through the EU Budget.

Scoreboard

Net Cost or Benefit	Net Cost
Most Likely Net Cost	1.5 per cent of GDP per year
Range of Estimates	1.2 to 1.7 per cent of GDP
Reliability of Estimate	A

The CAP, says the British Prime Minister, is a 'manifest absurdity'.[1] His Chancellor calls it a 'scandal'.[2] There can be little doubt that the CAP has inflicted serious damage on British agriculture, the British economy and, not least, on Third World countries.

With 16 per cent of EU-15 population and 18 per cent of EU-15 GDP,[3] the UK accounts for only 8.5 per cent of EU-15 agricultural output.[4] In contrast, the four big continental farming nations account together for over 65 per cent of EU-15 agricultural output (France 22.6 per cent, Italy 15.2 per cent, Germany 14.5 per cent, Spain 13.0 per cent). In France, Spain and Italy in particular, powerful electorally-influential farming lobbies frequently use violence against property and persons in pursuit of their perceived interests. The UK's very small share of EU-15 agricultural output, and the intense pressure from farming lobbies in big continental countries, ensure that, in EU-15's collective deliberations on the

10

CAP, British interests are largely ignored—just as they are when it comes to determining the EU stance in successive WTO 'rounds', when French intransigence in defending the CAP *à outrance* usually wins the day.

Despite being subject to the CAP, 19 per cent (see chapter 10, section 4, p. 47) of all UK imports of agricultural produce still comes from outside the EU. Under the EU Common External Tariff (CET) the UK is obliged to charge a tariff, currently averaging 11 per cent, on those imports. The UK tariff so collected (and forthwith handed over to the European Commission) accounts for no less than 43 per cent of the aggregated tariffs collected by all fifteen member states on their imports of agricultural produce from outside the EU. Not bad going for a country—the UK—that accounts for only 8.5 per cent of EU-15 agricultural output, but an indicator of the extent to which the CAP playing field is steeply tilted against the UK.

HM Treasury reports[5] that, for the whole of EU-15, the CAP costs 'EU taxpayers and consumers around $100 billion a year through subsidies and higher food prices', equivalent to 'an implicit tax on food of around 26 per cent'. The OECD[6] estimate for the EU-15 total is around 20 per cent higher than HM Treasury's: $119.4 billion, equivalent to 1.4 per cent of EU-15 GDP of $8,623 billion in 2002.[7]

The cost to British taxpayers and consumers is likely to be higher than the OECD estimate, for a number of reasons.[8] In particular, OECD figures exclude a number of categories of agricultural produce subject to substantial CAP intervention, such as fruit and vegetables, tobacco, cotton and wine. Moreover, British farmers do not—cannot—benefit significantly from subsidies on Mediterranean-type produce like tobacco, cotton or wine.

It seems safe therefore to estimate the total cost of the CAP to UK taxpayers and consumers at significantly above the 1.4 per cent of GDP derived from the OECD data. Conservatively, the range could be between 1.7 and 2.2 per cent of UK GDP.

Offsetting that is the 'benefit' of the effective producer subsidy received by British farmers, currently running at around £5 billion a year (see chapter 4),[9] (of which half is received back through the EU Budget, and half paid directly by HMG). That is equivalent to

0.5 per cent of GDP. To arrive at the *net* cost to the UK economy of the CAP, and to avoid double counting the CAP element in the EU Budget (chapter 4), that 0.5 per cent is subtracted from the total cost to UK taxpayers and consumers estimated above at between 1.7 and 2.2 per cent of GDP, to give a *net* range of between 1.2 and 1.7 per cent of GDP.

If the UK withdrew from the CAP, it is most unlikely that the remaining countries would abandon the CAP, given the leverage of the core countries' producer lobbies. In that scenario, since EU-14 (excluding the UK) agricultural output would be 91.5 per cent[10] of EU-15's (including the UK) the depressive effect of the CAP on world food prices[11] would continue, mitigated only marginally by the slight upward pressure on world prices as a result of extra demand from an ex-EU UK, free to source food tariff-free from the rest of the world. Assuming the UK would continue—at least in the medium term—to subsidise its own farmers at the same level that it does as an EU member, the net gain to the UK economy from leaving the CAP is equivalent to the net cost to the UK economy calculated above: between 1.2 and 1.7 per cent of GDP, amounting to between £12 billion and £17 billion a year at current levels of GDP.

Rock-bottom estimate

An absolutely minimal 'rock-bottom' net cost of the CAP can be estimated by taking HM Treasury's figure of $100 billion a year for the whole of EU-15, equivalent to 1.2 per cent of GDP, and making— however implausibly—the assumption that the impact of the CAP on the British economy is proportionately the same as the impact of the CAP on the economies of France, Spain, Italy and the other members of EU-15. In this scenario, netting off the half of one per cent of GDP in producer subsidy received by British farmers, the rock-bottom net cost of the CAP to the UK comes out at 0.7 per cent of GDP, or a rounded-down one half of one per cent of GDP.

4

The EU Budget

The UK pays 'Brussels' £4 billion more than it gets back. That £4 billion is a straight, hard direct subsidy to UK non-residents—a cost with no benefit.

Scoreboard

Net Cost or Benefit	Net Cost
Most Likely Net Cost	0.5 per cent of GDP per year
Range of Estimates	0.5 per cent of GDP upwards
Reliability of Estimate	AA

The EU Budget

Table 4.1
UK Net Transfers to EU Institutions

Year	£ billion
1993	3
1994	3
1995	5
1996	2
1997	3
1998	6
1999	5
2000	6
2001	3
2002	4
Cumulative	*40*
Annual Average	**4**

Source: *UK Balance of Payments: The Pink Book 2003, ONS.*

Transfers to and from 'EU Institutions' principally involve the Commission, which runs the EU Budget, and include the 'rebate' secured by Lady Thatcher at Fontainebleau in 1984.

This £40 billion, once it crossed the Channel, was spent by the Commission on subsidising the UK's competitors in EU-14, and in paying for the EU bureaucracy (Commission, Council, Parliament, Central Bank etc etc). A substantial proportion (no one knows how much) of the £40 billion of British taxpayers' money spent on the Continent was lost in fraud.

Analysing UK contributions to and receipts from the 'Community Budget' is complex.[1] In April 2003, HM Treasury published its annual 'statement on the EC Budget',[2] from which the following breakdown for the year 2002 is derived:

Table 4.2
UK Net Contribution to EC Budget: 2002

	£ bn	£ bn
All UK contributions to EC Budget	9.4	
Less Fontainebleau abatement	-3.1	
Gross UK contributions to EC Budget		*6.3*
All UK receipts from EC Budget		
Agricultural subsidies	-2.4	
Other receipts	-0.3	
Gross UK receipts from EC Budget		*-2.7*
Net UK contribution to EC Budget		*3.6*

Source: *European Community Finances: Statement on the 2003 EC Budget*, HM Treasury, Cm 5800, April 2003. www.hm-treasury.gov.uk

The net figure of £3.6 billion is £0.7 billion lower than the *Pink Book*[3] figure for 2002 of £4.3 billion. The additional net contribution of £0.7 billion results from private-sector payments, UK government payments to EU institutions other than the Commission, and UK contributions to EU aid programmes which are not counted as going to the EU Budget.

For the purposes of this paper the higher figure—£4.3 billion—is the relevant 2002 cost of the direct subsidy transferred from UK taxpayers to residents of EU-14 (and others). This is higher than the 1993-2002 average of £4 billion per year identified in Table 4.1 (p. 13). Rounded up to the level of accuracy used in this paper, the current net recurring cost is put at one half of one per cent of UK GDP.

This net cost is likely to be understated. It does not take into account the 'churn' impact—the 'frictional losses' of cycling large sums through the Brussels bureaucracy, with attendant losses from fraud and mismanagement, and the losses to UK welfare due to subsidies churned back to the UK being mainly deployed, through the command-economy mechanism of the CAP, as Brussels directs, not as the UK would have chosen had it been free to do so.[4]

Conclusion

The UK net contribution to Brussels is an ongoing pure cash transfer of the order of a minimum of 0.5 per cent of UK GDP, with no offsetting benefit. That figure is likely to be understated.

5

The Single Market

Net cost or benefit for the UK economy?

The Single Market came into effect in 1993. The dismantling of border controls on trade in goods, and the progressive freeing-up of trade in services and investment, has ·presumably brought economic benefits (difficult to discern); but also costs (measurable). Macroeconomic data and survey evidence suggest that the costs may outweigh the benefits. Many assert that the Single Market brings net benefits; but no convincing evidence exists that that is so.

Scoreboard

Net Cost or Benefit	Neutral to net cost
Most Likely Net Cost	Zero
Range of Estimates	Zero to negative
Reliability of Estimate	A

The Single Market (or 'internal market') is not and never will be complete. Nevertheless, the dismantling of most border controls for trade in goods, and the ongoing though painfully slow freeing-up of trade in services and investment, should on the face of it result in a benefit to member states' exporters, if not to other sectors of the economy. (It is worth noting that countries outside the EU can and do get such benefits through FTAs—including with the Single Market itself.)

However, the achievements of the Single Market programme come at a price. Arguably, the dismantling of border controls has simply replaced old-fashioned customs paperwork with a more cumbersome version: the fiendishly complicated VAT-based Intrastat forms which have to document every consignment of

16

goods crossing a national border (see UK business surveys, p. 8). More generally, the Single Market is inseparable from voluminous and detailed EU regulation, unequally-enforced across the EU, in products, markets, standards, health and safety, the environment and so on—all of which has to be imposed on the 90 per cent of the UK economy that is not involved in exporting to the Single Market, as well as the ten per cent that is (see Appendix II, p. 60). (Outside the EU, FTAs do not impose such costs.)

Consequently, though many assert that the Single Market delivers net benefits to the UK,[1] hard evidence that such is the case is non-existent. For example, the Bundesbank can find no evidence that it has helped German foreign trade.[2] The UK economy is unlikely to be any different. The Institute of Directors, in its 2000 publication,[3] reviewed studies from the Commission, the OECD and others and noted the absence of persuasive evidence of the benefits of the Single Market. Trade between EU member states and countries outside the EU is growing faster than trade between member states. The rate of growth of some larger non-EU countries' exports to the Single Market is higher than that of intra-EU exports.[4] Survey evidence (see UK business surveys, p. 8) indicates that some UK exporters believe that exporting to the Single Market is more costly than it was before the Single Market came into existence in 1993.

Despite (or because of?) the Single Market, EU-15's share of world trade has been shrinking. The ECB notes that data for 2003 'points to a loss in euro area export market share'. There is evidence that even within the EU-15 home market, non-EU firms are increasing their market share at the expense of 'domestic' firms. The general under-performance of the EU—particularly of the Eurozone and the Franco-German 'core'—is well documented in this paper and elsewhere.[5]

In the absence of any convincing evidence in the UK or elsewhere that the Single Market has actually delivered net benefits for the economies of member states, it is safe to conclude that at best its benefits and costs cancel each other out, and that at worst the costs could exceed the benefits by a considerable margin.

If the UK withdrew from the Single Market, what would be the impact on the British economy? Recent cost-benefit studies (See

Chapter 9, p. 36) suggest that the net impact would range between neutral and beneficial (i.e. being outside the EU is better than being inside). Other sections of this paper indicate that, if the UK left the EU, there would be zero economic impact on both inward investment (Chapter 6, p. 19) and tariffs (Chapter 10, p. 40), with, implicitly, a zero net impact for UK jobs.

The overall conclusion is that, inside the Single Market, the balance of costs and benefits for the UK economy is zero, that it could be negative, and that the UK would not suffer economically by being outside the Single Market.

6

The Importance of Inward Investment to the UK Economy

Net cost or benefit for the UK economy?

By international standards the level of inward investment into the UK is higher than average, but not exceptionally so. Such investment is overwhelmingly in the form of acquisitions and mergers, (as distinct from 'greenfield' investments in factories, whose impact at the macro level is modest). Little evidence exists that, overall, those acquisitions have a net benefit for the economy as a whole. Moreover, almost 80 per cent of inward investment is in UK services and oil and gas, where the 'access to the EU' question is irrelevant—as it is in most manufacturing investments.

Scoreboard	
Net Cost or Benefit	Neutral
Most Likely Net Cost	Zero
Range of Estimates	-
Reliability of Estimate	A

As noted elsewhere (see Appendix V, p. 66), the UK is one of the world's leading outward foreign direct investment (FDI) investors, and, at the same time, a leading recipient of inward FDI. How important or significant is that inward investment for the UK economy? Do its benefits outweigh its costs?

Table 6.1
UK Inward FDI flows v GFCF and v GDP

£ bn	1994	1995	1996	1997	1998	1999	2000	2001	2002	Average
FDI*	6	12.7	15.7	20.3	44.9	54.4	78.5	36.6	18.5	32
GFCF**	87	96	104	110	125	129	134	137	134	117
GDP†	681	719	763	811	859	904	951	994	1,044	858
FDI/GFCF	6.9%	13.2%	15.1%	18.5%	35.8%	42.2%	58.7%	26.6%	13.8%	27.4%
FDI/GDP	0.9%	1.8%	2.1%	2.5%	5.2%	6.2%	8.3%	3.7%	1.8%	3.7%

*   FDI inflows: Source: MA4: Foreign Direct Investment 2002, ONS, Feb 2004

** GFCF: (excludes new dwellings): Source: The Blue Book 2003, ONS, 2003

†   GDP @ current prices: Source: The Blue Book 2003, ONS, 2003

1. The 'macro' magnitudes

One indicator (approximate, because the numerator and denominator are statistically somewhat different) compares annual inward flows of FDI with all non-residential Gross Fixed Capital Formation (GFCF) in the economy. Another approximate measure compares FDI inflows with GDP. Table 6.1 shows the results.

On average, over the 1994-2002 period, FDI inflows accounted for just over a quarter of non-residential GFCF, though in the peak year 2000 the ratio approached 60 per cent. As a proportion of GDP, FDI flows varied from under one per cent in 1994 to over eight per cent in 2000. Superficially, such ratios appear to suggest that inward investment is important for the UK economy—though, when the form and make-up of FDI is examined (below), that conclusion may need revision.

Internationally, the UK ratios of FDI to GFCF and GDP are higher than the 'world' and 'developed countries' averages,[1] and higher than the ratios for developed economies of similar size, but not exceptionally so. Many smaller developed countries (for example Ireland and Sweden) have higher ratios than the UK.

2. The form of inward investment into the UK

For many people, 'inward investment' conjures images of foreign investors from the Far East building brand-new factories on greenfield sites. There are, of course, examples of that happening. But the reality is that direct investment in the UK is 'overwhelmingly in the form of acquisitions and mergers'[2](and very little comes from the Far East [see Table A5.1 in Appendix V, p. 66]).

Of itself, the acquisition of a British company by a foreign one does not create a single UK job or inject any capital into the underlying business. All that happens is that the shareholders of the British company receive cash and/or shares from the acquiror; those shareholders may or may not re-invest the proceeds by buying shares in other British companies. Those proceeds may not stay in the UK: after all, UK outward FDI is much bigger than inward FDI (see Appendix V, p. 67). When the acquiror and the acquiree are widely-held listed companies, the bulk of whose shareholders are usually Anglo-American financial institutions (fund managers, pension funds, insurance companies etc.) the transaction may boil down in those institutions' books to a slight re-shuffle of their holdings—again, with no job-creation or capital injection at the level of the acquired company's business.

An indication of the relatively minor effect on the UK economy of the 'greenfield' type of investment comes from *UK Trade and Investment* (formerly *invest.uk*), the government body (part of the Department of Trade and Industry) responsible for marketing the UK to inward investors. Its annual review 2003[3] reports that, excluding acquisitions, inward investment in 2002/2003 created 34,000 jobs in the UK economy. Welcome though those jobs are, they represent one eighth of one per cent of all UK jobs, so their impact at the macro level can only be modest.

Some acquisitions may result in an expansion of the business acquired; others may result in contraction ('rationalisation' in management-speak). For decades, research has suggested that more acquisitions damage shareholder value than enhance it. So while a high level of inward acquisitions of British companies may suggest that foreigners take a favourable view of the UK as a business location, it does not necessarily follow that taken as a whole those acquisitions are good for the British economy. All it may be indicating is that the UK has a liquid market in corporate control.

3. The make-up of inward investment into the UK

In 2002, based on earnings in that year alone on the cumulative inward investment made in the UK in the last couple of centuries, the breakdown by industry was as shown in Table 6.2. 'Manufacturing' accounted for 23 per cent of total earnings; 'services' 38 per cent and 'resources' (essentially oil and gas) 39 per cent.

'Access to the EU' plays no role in the decision of overseas investors to choose to invest in the UK in services and oil and gas. Moreover, 'access to the EU' may have been a factor—not necessarily decisive—in ten per cent or less of investments in UK manufacturing.[4] ('Access to the EU' cannot, by definition, explain the considerable inward investment in the UK that comes from other EU countries. [See table A5.1, in Appendix V, p. 66])

HM Treasury, in its October 1997 paper *UK Membership of the Single Currency: an Assessment of the Five Economic Tests*, said:

'The UK attracts a significantly larger share of inward investment than other countries in the EU. This reflects a number of important benefits that we offer, including low taxes, the English language and a flexible labour market.' Those benefits, it seems, do not include 'Europe'.

Table 6.2
Earnings by Industry

	Earnings* by industry (%)
Oil and Gas	39
Financial Services	18
Retail/Wholesale/Repairs	15
Mfr: Chemicals, plastics, fuel prods	10
Electr/gas/water distr.	7
Other industries	11
Total	*100*

* Earnings in 2002 on all inward investment.
Source: MA4: Foreign Direct Investment 2002: ONS, Feb 2004.

In 'Energy' ('Oil and Gas' plus 'Electric/gas/water distribution' in Table 6.2, accounting for 46 per cent of all inward investment), access to the Single Market is irrelevant. Oil and gas is a global industry (denominated in US dollars) whose commodity products are traded worldwide. EU-14 has no indigenous industry to 'protect'. North Sea reserves happen to be of high quality, located in a politically-stable part of the world and hence attractive to overseas investors. As for electricity generation and distribution, exchanges with the Continent are insignificant: there is only one electrical transmission cable under the Channel between England and France. Water distribution remains a purely British matter: there are no exchanges with the Continent. Whatever American and French and German companies are buying British generators and distributors for, it has nothing to do with access to the Single Market.

In Financial Services, accounting for 18 per cent of all inward investment, access to the Single Market is also irrelevant. This is another global industry whose products are mainly denominated in US dollars. Foreign companies invest in Britain because they need operations in the biggest, most liquid and most diverse financial centre in the world, the City of London (the reason for the strong German, French, Dutch, Swiss, Japanese and American presence) or because the UK market is attractive in itself (the reason why, for example, National Australia Bank bought Yorkshire Bank and Clydesdale Bank). If an American financial services group wants to operate in France, say, or Spain, it can and does invest there directly without going through the UK.

Inward investment in 'Distribution' ('Retail/Wholesale/ Repairs' in Table 6.2), accounting for 15 per cent of all inward investment, is largely unaffected by 'access to the Single Market'. Distribution companies may be finding benefits from reduced EU border controls (if they can avoid blockades by French truckers, fishermen and farmers); but it is difficult to think of any specific examples where the Single Market factor has been relevant, let alone decisive, in inward investment decisions into the UK distribution sector. A wealthy French businessman, François Pinault, did not buy Christies to get access to the Single Market. The US book retailer, Borders, did not buy *Books Etc* and start opening mega-stores throughout the UK to get access to the Single Market. Wal-Mart, the US giant, did not acquire Asda to get access to the Single Market. Thus, it is reasonable to conclude that 'access to the Single Market' is largely irrelevant in inward investment decisions into the British distribution sector.

This leaves the maximum 21 per cent (see Table 6.2: 'Mfr: Chemicals, plastics, fuel prods' plus 'Other industries'—the latter category may include some non-manufacturing activities as well) of all inward investment which goes into the British manufacturing sector.

Not belonging to the EU is palpably not a barrier to exporting physical goods to the EU, whose markets are awash with consumer and industrial products manufactured elsewhere, as a stroll through any factory, office, shop or market in any EU country shows.

Part of the reason is that geographical proximity to the consumer is no longer much of an issue in deciding where to locate manufacturing plant. (One example of this: bus seats on the number 88 London bus—the Clapham omnibus—are made in Australia.

Another example: Nissan cars made in Sunderland are sold in Australia.) In the past, the cost of freighting goods from manufacturer to consumer was significant in relation to the value of goods. Today, freight cost as a proportion of value is shrinking, as the speed and efficiency of air, sea and land transport increases. This is true not just of small items like semi-conductors, but of bulky and weighty objects like cars and locomotives. At the same time, the myriad back-up services which accompany the shipping of physical goods, such as bills of lading, engineering drawings, insurance and credit documentation, can be delivered instantaneously and cheaply via modern telecommunications, whose costs continue to fall steeply. Another part of the reason is that EU tariffs (chapter 10, p. 40) are already very low and tending to zero; the same is true of non-tariff barriers such as quotas.

Thus, as factors in decisions to locate manufacturing plant, neither geographical proximity to the end-consumer, nor tariff or non-tariff barriers, count for much. 'Access to the Single Market' is largely irrelevant for the non-manufacturing part of the economy and of minor and diminishing relevance in manufacturing itself.

4. FDI as a vector for the transmission of know-how

It is frequently argued that inward investment is one of the main vectors for the transmission of know-how from the investor country to the recipient country, and that the resulting 'spillover' improves domestic productivity. If this is so, then since British outward FDI is much greater than foreign investment inward into the UK, it would follow at the global level that the UK is a net exporter of know-how by the FDI transmission mechanism.

Nevertheless, recent research from the NIESR[5] (backing up research by Girma, Greenaway and Wakelin cited in *Better Off Out?*, (see chapter 9. p. 36), suggests that 'there is no clear pattern of benefits for domestic firms from the presence of foreign-owned firms. Indeed, spillovers are as likely to be negative as positive'.

Global mobility of middle and senior management, the use of English as the *lingua franca* of business, science, politics and much else, the near-universal use of the Internet and the centuries-old use of licensing arrangements are likely to be at least as important as FDI in transferring know-how internationally.

5. Conclusion

- The widely-held assumption that inward investment confers a net benefit on the UK economy is largely unsubstantiated

- The assertion that inward investment comes to the UK 'to get access to the rest of the EU'—the 'Gateway Theory'—has similarly never been substantiated

- It follows that, outside the EU, the UK economy would be no more nor less attractive to inward investors than it is at present.

7

Opportunity Cost

Net cost or benefit for the UK economy?

The economy of the continental EU, with which the UK is, in practice, obliged to 'converge', is seriously under-performing. Worse, the decline of continental EU, already apparent, looks set to continue. Could the UK have done better had it been free of the constraints of EU membership, and if so, how much better?

Even with rather modest assumptions about how much faster the economy of a UK outside the EU might have grown in the past, and might grow in the future, the cumulative effect in terms of percentage points of GDP ranges from six now to over twelve in the future.

Scoreboard

Net Cost or Benefit	Net cost
Most Likely Net Cost	6 per cent of GDP per year
Range of Estimates	6 per cent of GDP now, 12 per cent later
Reliability of Estimate	C

1. Ever closer union with a failing bloc

For over 30 years the whole of British government policy has been directed to 'integration' into and 'convergence' with the rest of the EU. In the economic field, the UK has enacted swathes of directives and regulations that impact heavily not just on the ten per cent or less of the economy actually involved in exporting to the EU, but also on the 90 per cent that is not.

Ever since 1973, as a member of the EU customs union, the UK's commercial policy has been that of the EC/EU, not one that the UK would have necessarily chosen had it been free to do so. For the last 15 years, the policy of successive British governments has been to join the euro 'when the time is right'. That policy is already influencing British economic management even though a referendum on the euro looks to be some years off. In agriculture, there is cross-party consensus that the CAP is, in Mr Blair's words, a 'manifest absurdity'[1]—but the UK must still apply it.

In the most recent ten years of the UK's 30-year EU membership it has become clear that the UK is busily 'integrating' itself into a regional bloc in relative decline. The economies of the EU as a whole, and of the Eurozone in particular, have under-performed. The reasons are complex. But whatever is causing such under-performance is what the whole of UK government policy is aimed at 'integrating' and 'converging' with.

So the 'counterfactual' question is: how would the UK have done, economically, had it not been in the EU? The gap between what actually happened, and what might have happened under different circumstances, would represent, for the UK, an opportunity cost.

2. What if?

What if the formidable energies and resources that the British government devotes to integration with 'Europe' had been diverted instead to standing free in the rest of the world? What if HM government had not had to spend much of the last ten years fending off the effects of the Working Time Directive, the Withholding Tax and much else and spent the time and energy instead on negotiating FTAs with the fastest-growing economies of the world, and with further liberalising the domestic economy itself?

'Opportunity cost', by definition, is not capable of 'proof'. That does not mean that the attempt to quantify it should not be made: on the contrary. There is no pre-destination about the fate of nations, as the example of Singapore shows. The 'what if' question has to be asked: the unthinkable thought. The task, however complex, is possible so long as reasoned judgements are made. A number of approaches suggest themselves.

One approach might be to look at sub-aspects of economic growth to identify why some countries do better than others. Extensive academic literature exists on the factors influencing economic growth, and the interaction between them. Correlations can be established for example between high levels of taxation and low growth, and vice-versa. Other factors include regulation of labour and product markets, trade protection, the educational system, capital investment (especially, seemingly, in IT) and the growth rates of a country's main trade and investment partners. These factors might be analysed over time as well. Perhaps the current under-performance of the main continental economies compared to the UK's is temporary. After all, thirty or forty years ago, the disparity in performance was the other way round. It is certainly within the bounds of possibility—just—that in, say, the next five years the British economy will decline and France and Germany recover. No one knows.

Another approach is to compare the actual performance of the UK with that of a peer group of non-EU economies with which the UK has particular affinities. One obvious peer group would consist of four mature advanced countries with predominantly English-speaking Anglo-Saxon-Celtic populations and constitutional, legal, educational and economic systems and cultures derived from British models. Those countries are the USA, Canada, Australia and New Zealand. (Ireland is also a candidate, but at least some of its quite remarkable performance in the last ten years can be ascribed to 'catching-up', unlike the four others.)

Three of the four chosen peer group countries have the same head of state as the UK; one, like the UK, is an offshore island with a temperate climate; another, the USA, is the UK's biggest single trading and investment partner. Two, geographically, are continental in size.

Table 7.1 shows the annual average compound rate of growth in real GDP of those countries between 1993, the year the Single Market began, and 2003, alongside that of the UK.

For mature economies such as these, growth rates of between three and four per cent are not exceptional. During that ten-year period 1993-2003, the rate of growth of the French economy exceeded three per cent three times. The US economy grew by more than three per cent in six of those ten years; the UK economy in four of those ten years. Compared with emerging countries like Korea, China and India, such rates of growth are quite modest. For the UK to have improved its growth rate from the 2.86 per cent it actually achieved between 1993 and 2003 to the 3.47 per cent achieved on average by the peer group would have meant increasing its growth rate by a fifth—not a particularly ambitious target.

Table 7.1
Annual Average Compound Rate of Growth in Real GDP,
1993 - 2003

	(%)
USA	3.24
Canada	3.52
Australia	3.76
New Zealand	3.35
Unweighted average of the above	*3.47*
UK	2.86

Source: Calculated from data in *OECD Economic Outlook*, December 2003, Statistical Annex, Table 1

3. The premise

The premise is that if the UK had been outside the EU, and been able to deepen its affinities with the Anglo-Saxon-Celtic peer group, its economy would have grown at the same average rate as the peer group between 1993 and 2003. If so, its real GDP in 2003 would have been 140.65 (indexed on 1993=100), 6.12 per cent higher than its actual real GDP in 2003 of 132.54 per cent (indexed on 1993=100). In other words, at the UK's present level of GDP of around £1,000 billion, had the UK grown at the same rate as the peer group, its economy would have been £60 billion bigger than it actually was.

That is just one estimate of the opportunity cost to the UK of being in the EU for a ten-year historical period. Is the EU as a whole likely to under-perform much of the rest of the developed world—let alone the emerging countries—in the next ten years as well? Here again a judgement has to be made. The European Commission certainly thinks so (p. 51). So do a number of respected non-British private- and public-sector bodies (p. 51). Re-casting the question, what is the likelihood of the core countries of the Eurozone (Germany, France and Italy together account for 70 per cent of Eurozone GDP) implementing enough radical economic reform in the next ten years to durably raise their growth rates? A dispassionate observer would probably say that for this to have any chance of happening a succession of Rosy Scenarios would have to be piled end-to-end. Any positive economic effect from EU enlargement will be counterbalanced by the substantial further transfers of power away from member states to the Brussels bureaucracy spelt out in numbing detail in the draft Constitution. The prognosis for the next ten years is not good.

The cumulative effect of low growth rates is like compound interest: small differences in growth rates amount eventually to quite large numbers. If, for example, the computation done above for the ten years from 1993 were extended to a 20-year period—in other words assuming that EU under-performance does not get any worse or better in the next ten years—then with the same assumed respective annual growth rates in real GDP of 2.86 per cent for the UK in the EU, and 3.47 per cent outside the EU, the difference in size of the UK economy at the end of the period would be 12.5 per cent, resulting in an opportunity cost in 2013 of £125 billion—annually—at today's values.

4. Conclusion

It is emphasised that opportunity cost or benefit is by definition uncertain. It rests on judgements. It is not capable of 'proof'—in contradistinction to direct costs, the calculation of which, though also involving a degree of judgement, is derived mainly from data measuring what actually happened. The estimate of opportunity cost made above is one way of quantifying the extra growth that the UK might—it is emphasised 'might'—gain from closer association with whatever it is that is delivering better performance for the peer group. Such opportunity benefit is additional to the direct costs that might be saved were the UK to leave the EU.

With those caveats it can be seen that even quite modest assumptions about the opportunity cost of UK membership in the last ten years alone indicate that the lost output could be significant: several percentage points of GDP. Over the next ten years, in the absence of radical reforms in continental EU, the opportunity cost for the UK could rise to a percentage of GDP in double figures—annually. Taking into account the cumulative effect of opportunities missed by virtue of EU membership in the 20 years between 1973 and 1992, and the possibility that the modest uplift in growth rate assumed between 1993 and 2003 might have been higher, the overall current opportunity cost could well be above six per cent of GDP.

8

Future Costs and Benefits
of EU Membership

Changes are in the EU pipeline that might affect the current balance between cost and benefit, which works out at a 'most likely' net ongoing cost (excluding opportunity cost) of four per cent of UK GDP.

Seven such pipeline measures are considered. In each case, the likely scenario is for an additional net cost for the UK.

1. EU constitution

British Government policy is to ensure that the Constitution be agreed and ratified in all 25 member-states as soon as possible. At the time of writing (summer 2004) the draft constitutional text runs to over 200 pages of prescriptive detail. The range of subjects covered is far wider than in the treaties (Rome to Nice) it replaces. The Charter of Fundamental Rights, about which British Ministers for Europe used to be so dismissive,[1] occupies a central place, and is to be legally binding and justiciable in the ECJ. In the words of a former Director-General for Financial Institutions and Company Law at the European Commission,[2] it is 'likely ... to diminish substantially member states' room for manoeuvre in reforming their labour markets and social security systems'.

It is highly probable that the Government's negotiating 'red lines' will prove to be as effective as the pre-war Maginot Line. They will fall, not to a frontal attack, but to 'judicial creep' through the European Court of Justice (ECJ)—as indeed has already happened in the tax field. Only the preternaturally naïve could read the EU Constitution and suppose that, following its enactment, the centralising and harmonising agenda of the regulatory bureaucracy in Brussels will be checked. The conclusion must be that, if and when the Constitution comes into force,

32

its impact on the existing net cost of UK membership of the EU will at best be neutral, and at worst significantly heavier.

2. Enlargement

Since most of the ten new member states have relatively low living standards and large agricultural sectors, pressure will probably build for higher subsidies than have already been budgeted by Brussels. Offsetting benefits are likely to be modest:[3] the combined GDP of the ten new members is roughly the same as Dutch GDP. If Romania, Bulgaria and a couple of the states formerly part of Yugoslavia join the EU shortly, the cost-benefit equation, especially as far as the UK, one of the richer states, is concerned, would probably tilt further in the direction of an increased net cost. When it comes to the accession of Turkey, with an exploding population already approaching that of Germany, the potential costs to the then 27 or 29 member-state EU, and to the UK, will be at least as substantial as the cost associated with the current wave of 12 to 15 acceding countries.

Theoretically, it is just conceivable that any economic benefits arising from EU enlargement will outweigh the costs. In practice—and the quasi-silence of the Commission and member-states' governments[4] on this topic is eloquent—it is difficult to envisage the impact on the existing net cost of UK membership of the EU being other than, at best, neutral, and at worst, more burdensome.

3. Abolishing sterling, adopting the euro

The stated, explicit and reiterated policy of the British Government is to adopt the euro 'when the five tests are judged (by HM Treasury) to have been met'—widely taken to be code for 'when a referendum can be won'. The Bank of England puts the net annual recurring cost of adopting the euro at one per cent or more of GDP, due to losing control of national monetary policy (à la ERM). The changeover costs of adopting the euro have been variously estimated at between three and four percentage points of GDP—between £30 billion and £40 billion at current GDP levels. Given that the actual benefits of having adopted the euro five years ago are still undetectable in Germany[5] (and probably elsewhere too), it would be reasonable to conclude that if the UK were to join, the costs would exceed the benefits and the existing net cost of UK membership of the EU would become more burdensome.

4. Tax harmonisation

The agenda of Brussels, France, Germany and other member-states is EU-wide tax harmonisation. That is precisely why one of the British Government's negotiating 'red lines' on the coming Constitution is to retain its veto on tax: a) because it believes tax harmonisation to be harmful, and b) because it fears the impact of the EU agenda. Notwithstanding, vetoes are already being overridden through judgements of the ECJ.[6] Tax harmonisation is happening; it cannot be stopped; and it will result in an increase, which is put by some observers at three per cent of GDP per year,[7] in the existing net cost of EU membership.

5. Ageing populations/pension crisis

Though all EU countries have ageing populations the problem is especially severe on the Continent, where, with the exception of the Netherlands, pay-as-you-go (i.e. non-funded) pension systems are the rule, and demography is particularly worrying.[8] As pension crises deepen, pressure will grow for EU-wide 'solidarity'—in practice, for UK taxpayers to help fund bankrupt continental systems.

The UK and Germany already massively subsidise the rest of the EU, especially continental farmers, through the mechanism of the EU Budget. So asking those countries to pay more would not exactly come as a surprise. Some argue that the Maastricht 'no bail-out' clause,[9] which in theory prevents one member-state bailing out another, would protect the UK from demands for pension subsidies. However, the precedent of the Growth and Stability Pact (GSP), whose legal base is (was) also in Maastricht, and which is (was) supposed to guarantee the stability of the single currency, is not encouraging. If push comes to shove, the bail-out clause will be shredded as ruthlessly and comprehensively as was the now-eviscerated GSP. The consequence could only be an increased net cost burden on the UK due to its EU membership, especially if by then the UK had joined the euro and consequently lost control of its own economy. Even if the bail-out clause remained operative, and continental member states funded their rising pension obligations by raising taxes, tax harmonisation (see above) would mean that an indirect burden fell on the British economy.

6. Social market regulation

Unemployment in the Eurozone, currently almost double that of the UK,[10] shows little sign of coming down. The timid national labour-market, pensions and healthcare reforms attempted in Germany and France[11] have left those countries with lame-duck governments. It has proved impossible to convince sufficiently large numbers of either their political leaders or their electorates that the continental social-market model is inferior to the Anglo-Saxon model. So it is that the failed social market model is now enshrined in the draft Constitution;[12] and so it is that the UK will eventually have to adopt its provisions, thus increasing the net cost to the UK of EU membership.

7. Opportunity cost

As noted in Chapter 7, on present trends, the opportunity cost of UK membership of the EU seems unlikely to decrease.

9

Recent Cost-Benefit Analyses

Three of the four extensive cost-benefit analyses done so far this century conclude that the net economic benefit for the UK of EU membership is—at best—marginal.

The fourth study, and a fifth currently under way, conclude that the current net cost for the UK of EU membership is substantial, and could rise steeply in future.

Four extensive EU cost-benefit exercises have so far been carried out by long-established organisations in the present century. In February 2000, the (British) National Institute of Economic and Social Research (NIESR) published *'Continent Cut Off? The Macroeconomic Impact of British Withdrawal from the EU'*.[1] The paper was commissioned by *Britain in Europe*, the government-sponsored lobbying group. The (British) Institute of Directors (IoD) published *EU Membership: What's the Bottom Line?*,[2] by its chief economist, in March 2000. In August 2000, the (US) International Trade Commission (ITC), a federal non-partisan agency of the US government, published *The Impact on the US Economy of Including the United Kingdom in a Free Trade Arrangement with the United States, Canada and Mexico*,[3] in which it examined two scenarios, the UK joining NAFTA and staying in the EU, and the UK joining NAFTA and leaving the EU. In 2001, the (British) Institute of Economic Affairs (IEA) published *Better Off Out?*,[4] an updated version of their original paper which first came out in 1996.

None of the four papers can be accused of bias on the European question. All rely on objective data and, where assumptions have to be made—which they inevitably do—on judgements made in good faith. The American study, concentrating on the interests of the US economy, can be considered to be impeccably neutral on the question of UK membership of the EU. The NIESR is a non-partisan body, though occasionally leaning to the pro-EU side of the spectrum. The IoD, one of the British business world's two main membership organisations, reflects and promotes the views of its members; lately, it is fair to say, those views have sometimes tended to euroscepticism. The authors of the IEA paper have published books and papers critical of aspects of the EU.

Given their different perspectives, it is striking that three of the four studies—those of the NIESR, the ITC and the IEA—reach broadly similar conclusions. These are that the economic impact of British withdrawal from the EU would be marginal—less than one per cent of GDP. Putting it another way, these three studies find that, for the UK, the net economic benefits of EU membership are at best marginal.

All three studies looked at the UK, the EU and the world 'as is'. They assume, implicitly, that the impact of the EU on the British economy will get neither better nor worse; that the UK will stay out of the euro; that the regulatory burden (if such it is) of being in the EU is minor; and that the respective demographic and economic weights and influence in the world of the UK and the EU will not change over time. None took account of the opportunity cost of EU membership.

The NIESR assumed that inward investment has a major positive impact on overall British productivity and that inward investment would fall significantly if the UK left the EU. The American study found that the net effect on inward investment would be zero. The IEA, discussing inward investment and British welfare, raised the possibility that on balance it makes the UK worse off. The NIESR assumed that, outside the EU, British exporters to the EU would have to surmount an effective tariff barrier of nine per cent; the IEA postulated about six per cent. The American position was that, in or out of the EU, 'tariff and other trade barriers between the UK and the North American countries are already rather low'.

The NIESR study, discussing the number of UK jobs associated with exports to the EU, states unequivocally that 'there is no *a priori* reason to suppose that many of these [jobs], if any, would be lost permanently if Britain were to leave the EU'. The study finds that post-withdrawal there would be more jobs in the British economy in the medium term than if Britain stayed in. A similar conclusion can be inferred from the American study, which, in the scenario where the UK leaves the EU completely, finds that UK domestic output—and presumably employment—is stimulated in 'mining, iron and steel, other manufacturing and services', thus cutting the deficit with the EU.

The IoD study is the only one of the four which comes up with a more-than-marginal current net cost of EU membership, and looks beyond the 'as is' scenario to the future. On inward investment, it assumes a current benefit to the UK of EU membership of around 0.5 per cent of GDP per annum. It assumes that being in the EU customs union results in a benefit of 0.5 per cent of GDP. Offsetting this total one per cent benefit are costs of 2.75 per cent of GDP (of which EU Budget 0.75 per cent, CAP one per cent and 'social model' one per cent). Overall, the IoD estimates that the *minimum* net cost to the UK is 1.75 per cent of GDP, but that it might be as much as three per cent. (Based on the 2003 level of GDP that would translate as a current minimum annual cost of £17.5 billion and a possible cost of £30 billion.)

Allowing for the likely future consequences of further 'integration' within the EU, the IoD concluded that through EU tax harmonisation alone (still the official policy of the Commission and the French government[5]) the annual cost could double to around six per cent of GDP—£60 bn a year at today's level of GDP. That is without counting the cost of joining the euro, which, in terms of loss of output due to loss of control of monetary policy, *à la ERM*, is estimated by the Bank of England[6] to be one per cent or more of GDP—another £10 billion at today's level of GDP.

It is worth noting that a fifth study, by Professor Minford and Vidya Mahambare, is presently under way at Cardiff University. An interim 'progress report' was published in the form of an article[7] in September 2003. This also looks at the future as well as the present. Its preliminary conclusion is that the net cost to the UK of EU membership is substantial.

The results of these five twenty-first century cost-benefit analyses should surprise no-one. Well before 1973, when the UK actually joined the then Common Market, economists concluded that the economic impact on the UK of EC accession would be unequivocally negative. That was the finding of John Murray's paper[8] for Hugh Gaitskell (an early Labour eurosceptic) in 1959, and, in the late 60s and early 70s, of Kaldor, Miller/Spencer, and Josling-Williamson.[9] Even the 1970 and 1971 White Papers predicted negative economic consequences. *Plus ça change, plus c'est la même chose* ...

Conclusion

None of the four major studies indicates that membership of the EU results in a more-than-marginal net economic benefit for the UK of EU membership. The estimates of net cost to the UK range from 'marginal' to £60 billion—not counting the cost of joining the euro. The Cardiff exercise—not yet finished—points to a significant net cost.

Were the NIESR and IEA exercises to be re-run, assuming firstly average tariff barriers in line with actual current levels (see chapter 10) for UK exporters to the EU, and secondly a lower benefit to the UK from inward investment (see chapter 6), it is possible that they too would result in more-than-marginal levels of net cost to the UK of belonging to the EU.

10

The UK in the World Trading System[1]

Free trade between the UK and the EU would continue if the UK were outside the EU. Most World Trade Organisation (WTO) members, including those with higher living standards than almost all EU countries, choose to organise their international trade via free trade agreements (FTAs) rather than customs unions like the EU's.

Overall, in terms of their members' economic performance, evidence of the superiority of customs unions over FTAs is hard to detect.

With tariffs now so low, the notion that a country's trade—especially that of the third-biggest trading country on the planet, the UK—would not thrive outside the EU customs union is far-fetched.

1. Free trade between the UK and the EU would continue if the UK were outside the EU

If the UK withdrew from the EU it would be in the interests of both parties—especially the remaining EU—to negotiate arrangements providing for bilateral trade as free as, or more free than, they enjoy at present.

The reasons are as follows. First, ever since 1997, trade-in-goods between 30 European nations, including all 25 EU member-states, has in effect been tariff-free, under the PESCO (see section 2 below). Trade-in-goods between the EU and the rest of the world is still subject to tariffs, but at very low average levels (see section 3 below). Following UK withdrawal, neither the remaining EU nor the UK would be able, under WTO rules on 'tariff-binding' (section 3 below), to erect tariff barriers against each other higher than presently exist between the EU (including the UK) and the rest of the world. Nor would they wish to.

Second, on its trade-in-goods with the UK, EU-14 runs a structural, perennial surplus.[2] Looked at through the other end of the telescope, the UK is in structural perennial deficit on its trade-in-goods with EU-14: it buys more from EU-14 than it sells to EU-14.

Table 10.1
EU-14 Surplus on its Exchanges with the UK: £ bn

Year	Balance: Trade in Goods Services & Income	Balance: Transfers to and from EU Institutions	Overall Balance
1993	5	3	8
1994	5	3	8
1995	4	5	9
1996	3	2	5
1997	-1	3	2
1998	-4	6	2
1999	4	5	9
2000	-1	6	5
2001	-2	3	1
2002	11	4	15
Cumulative	*24*	*40*	*64*
Annual Average	**2.4**	**4**	**6.4**

Source: *UK Balance of Payments: The Pink Book 2003, ONS.*

In 2002, the UK goods deficit with EU-14 was £20 billion. In that year, Germany sold the UK almost £1.50-worth of goods for every pound's-worth that the UK sold to Germany, resulting in a German surplus on its goods trade with the UK of £10 billion. Neither EU-14, nor its member-states, would wish to put those surpluses at risk by erecting trade barriers between themselves and the UK. To put it bluntly, the EU, with its millions of unemployed, needs the UK more than the UK needs the EU.

Third, the UK is by far EU-14's biggest single customer for goods (section 5 below), well ahead of the USA in that respect.

Again, post-withdrawal, EU-14 would not wish to discriminate against its single biggest customer.

Fourth, the EU-14's foreign direct investment (FDI) in the UK is substantial; so is the UK's in EU-14 (see Appendix IV, p. 64). The profit-earning (and job-creating) capacity of such FDI is partially sustained by the quasi-absence on both sides of the Channel of tariff and non-tariff barriers to trade. Neither a UK outside the EU, nor the remaining EU, would wish to put such FDI at risk by raising new trade barriers between them.

Fifth, the UK is not only EU-14's biggest customer: it is the world's third-biggest trading nation (see Appendix I, p. 55) after the USA and Germany. Post-UK withdrawal, the interests of EU-14 (by then possibly EU-26 or 28) in general, and Germany, the world's second-biggest trading nation in particular, would be best served by retaining barrier-free trade with the third-biggest trading nation.

For all these reasons, the often-brandished scenario of a post-withdrawal UK 'isolated' from the Continent, friendless, having to export into that Continent over a penal tariff barrier, is absurd. Straightforward uncomplicated mutual commercial self-interest would rapidly assert itself over any initial petulance and ensure that, post-withdrawal, UK-EU trade would be as free, if not more so, than it is now.

2. Free trade agreements are the future, customs unions the past

Of the two hundred or so nation-states in the world, approximately 175 manage perfectly well to trade internationally without being part of the EU customs union. On many measures (see Appendix III, p. 62) a number of them do rather better than EU countries—not just when trading outside the EU but even within the EU. International comparisons, and the fact that countries are increasingly choosing to conduct trade via free trade agreements (FTAs) rather than customs unions, (which, apart from the EU's, are mainly confined to developing countries in Africa and South America) lend little support to the view that an EU-type customs union is the best way to organise intra- and extra-customs union trade—rather the contrary. In fact, FTAs look to be the trend of the future.

Trade between those approximately 175 nation-states outside the EU, and those states' trade with the EU itself, is largely carried out within the framework of bilateral, regional and cross-regional free trade agreements (FTAs) which, (like customs unions such as the EU's), conform to the rules of, and are subject to oversight by, the World Trade Organisation (WTO). By the end of 2002, a total of 259 regional trade agreements had been notified to the WTO;[3] a further 70 were in operation but not yet notified. Another 60 FTAs were in negotiation. Only four WTO members, all small Asian countries, were not party to a regional FTA; soon, the bulk of world trade in goods will occur under the umbrella of regional FTAs.

Already, by the mid-1990s, 13 of the accession countries of Central and Eastern Europe, including the ten which joined the EU in May 2004, plus Bulgaria, Romania and Turkey, had signed FTAs (known as 'Europe Agreements') with the EU. In 1997 these FTAs were combined into the Pan-European System of Cumulation of Origin (PESCO),[4] administered jointly by EFTA[5] and the EU. The PESCO, with, currently, 25 EU members and five non-EU members, has already resulted in the creation of a pan-European free trade zone in goods (approximately two-thirds of cross-border trade in Europe is in goods). If one or more countries withdrew from the EU, they would continue to be part of the PESCO, simply shifting into the non-EU group of PESCO members like Switzerland, Norway and Turkey.

Outside the EU, the UK would rapidly insert itself into the fast-growing interlocking global network of FTAs. Whether inside or outside the EU, the UK, the third-biggest trading nation in the world after the USA and Germany (see Appendix I, p. 55), would continue to be a WTO member and trade internationally within the WTO framework.

The main difference is that, inside the EU, the UK has no seat at the WTO table, no vote in its deliberations and no ability to strike up alliances with major like-minded trading partners such as the USA or Australia (which, incidentally, signed a comprehensive bilateral FTA[6] in March 2004). The British government can influence the EU Trade Commissioner (currently the Frenchman, Pascal Lamy) who negotiates at the WTO on behalf of the member-states, but it only has one voice amongst 25. Outside the EU, the UK would resume its own seat and vote at the WTO, its leverage in keeping with its position as the third-biggest trading nation —'cutting out the EU middleman' as it were. UK leverage at the WTO is sometimes claimed to be stronger as part of the EU customs union than it would be if the UK spoke for itself in WTO councils. That claim has validity only in so far as British commercial interests coincide with those of all or a majority of its EU partners—all 24 of them. When British interests do not so coincide, it follows that UK leverage is weaker than it would be if the UK were outside the EU.

Given that the structure and pattern of UK global trade (see Appendix I, p. 55) is quite different from that of its EU partners, there is no *a priori* reason to suppose that, on balance, British interests and those of its EU partners coincide more often than they diverge. Many argue that French intransigence in defending the indefensible, the CAP, not only introduces long delays into successive WTO 'rounds', including the Uruguay Round of the 1990s and the current Doha Round, but ensures that their outcomes are far from being what the UK (and others) would have wanted.

An assessment of whether, on balance, the UK gains or loses through having neither voice nor vote at the WTO is beyond the scope of this paper. It should be noted however that in the United Nations, the World Bank and the International Monetary Fund, the other main global institutions set up after the Second World War at the same time as the WTO's predecessor, GATT, the UK shows no inclination to surrender its votes and seats to functionaries—however brilliant—of a regional bloc. Neither does it do so in a regional security body, NATO.

Outside the EU, the UK would therefore be able, within the WTO framework, to negotiate FTAs with other countries, and with customs unions such as the EU. (A NAFTA member, Mexico, which signed an FTA[7] with the EU in 1999, gains the same access to the Single Market as EU members themselves, with few, if any, of the costs.) The UK might choose to trade with countries without having FTAs with them. (At present, the UK trades with its single biggest trading and investment partner, the USA, without an FTA, since the EU and the USA have no bilateral FTA.) The UK would also be able, if it so chose, to apply to join multi-country FTAs such as NAFTA, which presently comprises the USA, Canada and Mexico.

3. Tariffs: now so low as to be hardly worth collecting

Cross-border trade consists of trade in goods, trade in services, and receipts of income (on income-generating assets such as direct and portfolio investments, and financial assets such as loans or deposits). Transfers such as payments to and receipts from supranational (e.g. the EU) or multilateral (e.g. the UNO) organisations, and remittances by residents of one country to residents of another country, are also included in the balance-of payments definition of trade. 'Goods' or 'merchandise' are called 'visibles'; all the other categories of trade, including transfers, are called 'invisibles'.

Exports of goods by all countries in 2002 accounted for 66 per cent of total exports, exports of invisibles for 34 per cent (see Appendix I, p. 55). For the UK, exports of goods accounted for well under half—46 per cent—of its total exports (Appendix I).

Tariffs, also known as customs duties, are taxes levied on imports of goods only. Trade in many categories of goods—perhaps accounting for half[8] of global trade in goods by value—is tariff-free. Trade in invisibles—services, income and transfers—is tariff-free. Approximately two-thirds of all global trade in visibles and invisibles is thus already likely to be completely tariff-free.

Non-tariff barriers to trade in both visibles and invisibles tend to be low in industrialised countries (except on agricultural products) and high in some developing countries.

Average tariffs on trade in goods amongst developed countries are already low. The *2004 Index of Economic Freedom*[9] lists the 'common EU weighted average external tariff' in 2001 as 2.6 per cent. The weighted average tariff in 2001 for the USA was listed as 1.8 per cent; Japan's as 2.1 per cent; Canada's as 0.9 per cent; Mexico's as 1.7 per cent; Australia's as 3.9 per cent; Estonia's (in 2002) as 0.05 per cent; Norway's as 1.6 per cent. Listed as 'approximately zero' were those of Switzerland, Singapore and Hong Kong. These tariff estimates are believed to be theoretically calculated, and higher than, rates of tariff calculated by dividing duties actually collected by the value of imports.

Based on actual amounts of tariff collected,[10] the average tariff (CET—'Common External Tariff') on imports of goods into EU-15 from non-EU countries in 2002 worked out at 1.5 per cent. For the UK, the average tariff was 1.9 per cent; for EU-14, 1.4 per cent. Average tariff rates within EU-15 varied in 2002 from 2.4 per cent for Belgium to 0.8 per cent for Ireland. For Germany the rate was 1.3 per cent; for France, 1.3 per cent; for Italy, 1.3 per cent. The variations were presumably due to the varying 'mix' in different countries' overall imports of goods from outside the EU.

Since most EU-15 countries import more than half their goods completely tariff-free from other member-states, their effective tariff rates on all imports of goods from inside and outside the EU are much lower: under one per cent.

In the case of the UK (see section 4 below), 85 per cent of its goods imports from inside and outside the EU are already tariff-free. Its overall tariff rate on all imports of goods from outside and inside the EU is below one per cent: 0.8 per cent. On its imports of goods from outside EU-14, the UK bore an average tariff of 1.9 per cent (1.6 per cent excluding agricultural and fishing produce).

WTO members' tariffs are 'bound' at ceiling rates above which they can never normally be increased; the introduction of quotas or other trade-restricting measures is similarly not normally permitted.[11] Thus, if an EU member state were to withdraw from the EU customs union, then, even in the absence of a bilateral FTA between the parties, the then-current tariff rates of the withdrawing state, and those of the remaining EU member states, would continue to be 'bound' at their previous levels, unless they, and the EU itself, withdrew from the WTO (something no WTO or GATT member has ever done). Those average ceiling rates are now so low—around one per cent—as to be hardly worth collecting.

The aim of successive GATT/WTO trade 'rounds'—Uruguay in the 1980s and 1990s, Doha currently—is to reduce tariff and non-tariff barriers even further. In parallel, in the WTO, EFTA, the EU and other global and regional bodies, work goes on in 'trade facilitation'—standardising and simplifying customs paperwork, computerisation, delivering export documentation electronically etc. This also is reducing the cost of trading internationally. Thus, the cost of exporting as a proportion of the value of goods exported continues to fall, irrespective of the level of tariff rates.

Table 10.2
2002: UK Tariffs on Imports of Goods: £ bn

From where	Imports	CET*	Average Tariff Rate (%)
Outside EU: industrial goods	100.1	1.60#[12]	1.6
Outside EU: agr. +fish produce	2.8[13]	0.3[14]	10.9
Outside EU: all goods	**102.9[15]**	**1.91**	**1.9**
EU-14: industrial goods	117.8	zero	zero
EU-14 agr. + fish produce	12.1	zero	zero
EU-14 all goods	**129.9[16]**	**zero**	**zero**
World: industrial goods	217.8	1.6	0.7
World: agr. +fish produce	14.9[17]	0.3	2
Total from World	**232.7[18]**	**1.91**	**0.8**

*   the EU Common External Tariff—'CET'
\#   of which £9.5 million as EU Anti-Dumping Duties[19]

4. UK imports of goods and tariffs thereon

- Of the £426 billion of all UK imports (goods, services, income and transfers) in 2002, no less than £391 billion, or 92 per cent, were tariff-free

- Of the £232.7 billion value of total UK imports of *goods* from the world (EU-14 and outside the EU) in 2002, no less than 85 per cent (£198.1 billion) bore a zero tariff

- The remaining 15 per cent by value of total UK imports of *goods* (£34.6 billion—all imported from outside the EU) bore an average tariff of 5.5 per cent

- Within that average tariff of 5.5 per cent, imports of *industrial goods* (excluding agricultural and fishing produce) from outside the EU bore an average tariff of 1.6 per cent, while imports of *agricultural and fishing produce* from outside the EU bore an average tariff of 10.9 per cent

- In 2002, as a proportion of the value of total UK imports of goods (industrial and agricultural and fishing produce) from the world (EU-14 and outside EU-14), the average tariff was 0.8 per cent.

Figure 10.1
92 per cent by Value of All UK Imports were Tariff-free in 2002

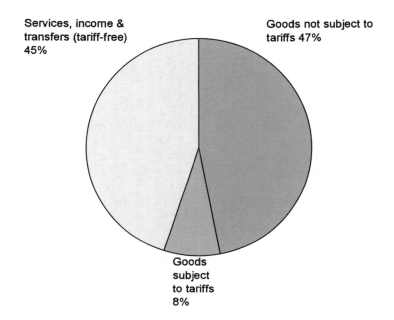

Services, income &
transfers (tariff-free)
45%

Goods not subject to
tariffs 47%

Goods
subject
to tariffs
8%

Table 10.3
2002: Tariffs by Tariff Bands: UK Imports of Goods: £ bn

From where	Imports	Imports Indexed	CET*
Outside EU: industrial: positive tariff	31.8	*32*	1.61
Outside EU: industrial: zero tariff	68.3	*68*[20]	zero
Outside EU: industrial total	100.1	*100*	1.61
EU-14: industrial: zero tariff	117.8		zero
Outside EU; agr.+fish produce: positive tariff	2.8		0.30
EU-14: agr.+fish produce: zero tariff	12.1		zero
World: industrial & agr.+fish produce	**232.7**[21]	*100*	**1.91**
of which: positive tariff	34.6	*15*	1.91
zero tariff	198.1	*85*	zero

*   the EU Common External Tariff—'CET'

5. The UK's importance as a customer (market) for the EU

The UK is EU-14's biggest single customer, ahead of the USA (Table 10.4).

Table 10.4
2002: EU-14: Exports of Goods, Services and Income Receipts

To the UK	£208 bn	*Source: The Pink Book 2003*
To the USA	£191 bn*	*Source: US Balance of Payments*

* Converted at the average 2002 exchange rate of £1 = $1.50 (Source: ECB)

The UK is also the Eurozone's (EU-14 less Denmark and Sweden) biggest single customer (Table 10.5), absorbing about a fifth of the Eurozone's exports.

Table 10.5
2002: Eurozone: Exports of Goods*

To the UK	€206 bn	*Source: ECB Monthly Bulletin Feb. 2004*
To the USA*	€184 bn	*Source: ECB Monthly Bulletin Feb. 2004*

* Data on a current account basis (including goods, services, income and transfers) not available on a comparable basis; but it is likely that the UK is also the Eurozone's biggest customer on this basis.

Reliability Rating: AA

11

The Coming Decline of the EU?

Profound shifts in global power, influence and prosperity are in prospect. American predominance will continue; new powers will rise in Asia. European governments (including Mr Blair's), the Commission, economists and historians agree that the decline of continental EU has begun, and will deepen.

1. Demography

World population was 6.1 billion in 2000.[1] By 2050 it is expected to be 9.3 billion. In 2050, as in 1950 and 2000, the three most populous countries in the world will be India (1.6 billion), China (1.5 billion) and the USA (0.4 billion). The population of developed countries, currently 1.2 billion, is expected to change little. By 2050, the populations of 39 countries are expected to be smaller than today, the five biggest decreases being in Russia, Ukraine, Japan, Italy and Germany.

The working-age population of the EU, even after its current enlargement to 25 members, is projected[2] to decline by 20 per cent to 30 per cent by 2050. The severest losses will be in Italy and Spain; the UK's working-age population is expected to grow slightly. Meanwhile, the working-age population of the USA will increase by almost a third.

- By 2050, the working-age population of the USA will have increased by more than the entire present working-age population of Germany

- EU-15, in contrast, will have lost almost as much working-age population as the entire present working-age population of Germany

- Only two EU-15 nations (apart from Luxembourg) are projected to experience growth in working-age population by 2050: Ireland and the UK, both English-speaking offshore islands

- The further east one goes in Europe, the worse demography gets. All ten nations that joined the EU in 2004, plus Romania and Bulgaria, are projected to suffer losses in working-age population by 2050, ranging from slight (Cyprus, Malta) to awful (Bulgaria, Latvia and Estonia)

- By 2050, the combined working-age population of Russia, Ukraine and Belarus will have shrunk by 46 per cent

- Turkey's working-age population is projected to grow by two-fifths by 2050

- Japanese working-age population is projected to shrink by 38 per cent by 2050

- In 2050, the median age of the US population will be the same as that of the EU-15 today

- The median age of the EU-15 population will increase from 38 in 2000 to almost 50 in 2050

A separate study,[3] which made projections out to 2030, highlighted the following:

- Italy's retirees will outnumber its active workers by 2030

- Germany and Mexico today have working-age populations of about 50 million. By 2030, Mexico will have twice as many working-age people as Germany

- The 335 million working-age people that India is expected to add by 2030 approaches the total working-age populations of the entire EU and the USA combined in 2000.

2. From demographics to economics

The decline of the EU, already begun, will accelerate in the decades to come. That, in essence, is the stated view of, amongst others:

- Mr Blair, Mr Chirac and Mr Schröder[4]
- Mr Zalm, Dutch Finance Minister[5]
- Dr Denis McShane, the UK's Minister for 'Europe'[6]
- HM Treasury[7]
- The European Commission

- Messrs McRae, Kaletsky, Bootle, Taylor, Coutts, Professor Rowthorn, Miss Lea and others[8]
- Mr Niall Ferguson, the British historian[9]
- French authors Nicolas Baverez, Professor Jean-Paul Fitoussi, Professor Alain Cotta[10]
- Mr Robert Kagan.[11]

Established well-resourced mainstream bodies have reached similar conclusions. They combine projections of change in employment (i.e. working-age populations) with assumptions about—amongst other factors—rates of change in capital accumulation, import/export elasticity and total factor productivity, to produce estimates of countries' GDP and trade.

In one such study, the European Commission itself takes a gloomy view of the EU's prospects.[12] In its December 2002 review of the EU economy, it says '... *the EU has already witnessed a steady erosion in its share of global output, a trend which is forecast to continue over the coming decades ... the EU will be badly affected by ageing* ...' It forecasts a 44 per cent decline in the EU-15 share of global GDP from 18 per cent in 2000 to ten per cent in 2050, along with a 13 per cent increase in US share in the same 50 years from 23 per cent to 26 per cent.

Another study, *Le Commerce Mondial au 21e Siècle: Scénarios pour l'Union Européenne*,[13] commissioned by the European Commission from the Institut Français des Relations Internationales (IFRI), is equally pessimistic. Its base scenario, containing projections of GDP and world trade to 2050, is entitled '*Chronicle of a Decline Foretold*'. Its projections are not dissimilar from those of the European Commission. EU-30 (EU-15 plus the ten states joining in 2004, plus Romania, Bulgaria and three Balkan states, but excluding Turkey) is projected to suffer a loss in share of global GDP from 22 per cent in 2000 to 12 per cent in 2050. Meanwhile, NAFTA maintains its 24 per cent share and Greater China increases share from nine per cent to 24 per cent. The authors admit that their assumptions about EU productivity growth are 'very optimistic'. Concludes IFRI, in its English-language summary: '... *the EU will have an ever-decreasing influence on the course of globalisation; its chapter in world history will draw to a slow but inexorable close*'. (In the original French it sounds even more dramatic: '*une lente mais inexorable sortie de l'Histoire est envisageable*').

Goldman Sachs, a leading investment bank, in an October 2003 research paper,[14] also suggests that huge shifts in global economic power will have come about by 2050. By then (Table 11.1) China will be the biggest economy in the world, having overtaken the UK in 2005, Germany in 2007, Japan in 2016 and the USA in 2041. America, in 2050, will be the second biggest and India the third biggest economy in the world.

Table 11.1
Real GDPs Indexed on UK = 100

2003		2050	
USA	695	China	1180
Japan	279	USA	930
Germany	121	India	735
UK	*100*	Japan	176
France	89	Brazil	161
China	86	Russia	155
Italy	74	*UK*	*100*
India	33	Germany	95
Brazil	29	France	83
Russia	27	Italy	54

Source: Wilson, *Dreaming With BRICS: The Path to 2050*; Global Economics Paper No. 99, 2003. www.gs.com

3. The consequences of economic decline

- Growth in GDP, market size and equity returns will tend to occur outside Europe

- The EU Single Market will be a shrinking market, unattractive to investors

- The tax base will shrink; tax rates and debt will have to increase

- Shrinking and ageing populations mean more demand for healthcare and pensions with fewer people to provide them

- Most EU countries will see falling demand for houses, schools, factories and shops, with falling asset values and investment. This will affect the financial and equity markets on which pension provision depends

- The process of assimilating immigrants will become more problematic

- Sharply-diverging demographics within the EU will make EU-wide one-size-fits-all policies (monetary, tax, labour-market, agricultural, asylum, immigration, environmental etc.) even more inappropriate

- The economic rationale of 'integration' into a fading regional bloc, the EU, a contracting market for UK (and other) exporters, will become even more questionable.

Reliability Rating: C

Appendix I

The World's Seven Biggest Exporting Nations

Table A1.1
$US bn: Exports ('credits on current account'): 2002

Rank	Country	Goods	Services	Income	Transfers	Totals
1	USA	685	289	256	11	**1,241**
2	Germany	615	106	103	16	**840**
3	*UK*	*279*	*125*	*186*	*17*	*607*
4	Japan	396	66	91	10	**563**
5	France	306	87	81	19	**493**
6	Italy	254	60	43	21	**378**
7	Canada	264	37	20	5	**326**
	Rest of World	3,567	852	483	326	**5,228**
	World	**6,369**	**1,622**	**1,263**	**422**	9,676
	World %	*66%*	*17%*	*13%*	*4%*	*100%*

Source: *IMF Balance of Payments Statistics Yearbook 2003*, (www.imf.org). The data has not been adjusted for the Rotterdam-Antwerp Effect (Appendix IV) or the Netherlands Distortion (Appendix V).

Table A1.2
Market Shares of Word Exports

Country	(%)
USA	12.8
Germany	8.7
UK	*6.3*
Japan	5.8
France	5.1
Italy	3.9
Canada	3.4
Rest of World	54.0
World	**100.0**

Note: Derived from Table A1.1
Source: *IMF Balance of Payments Statistics Yearbook 2003*, (www.imf.org). The data has not been adjusted for the Rotterdam-Antwerp Effect (Appendix IV) or the Netherlands Distortion (Appendix V).

Table A1.3
Exports by type: 2002: Percentages

Country	Goods	Invisibles*	Total
USA	55	45	100
Germany	73	27	100
UK	*46*	*54*	*100*
Japan	70	30	100
France	62	38	100
Italy	67	33	100
Canada	81	19	100
Rest of World	68	32	100
World	**66**	**34**	**100**

Note: Derived from Table A1.1
* Invisibles = Services + Income + Transfers
Source: *IMF Balance of Payments Statistics Yearbook 2003*, (www.imf.org). The data has not been adjusted for the Rotterdam-Antwerp Effect (Appendix IV) or the Netherlands Distortion (Appendix V).

Table A1. 4
Leading Countries' Shares of World Exports*

Country	1996 Share %	2002 Share %	Change 2002 v 1996
USA	13.5	12.8	(5%)
Germany	8.8	8.7	(1%)
UK	*6.5*	*6.3*	*(3%)*
Japan	7.3	5.8	(21%)
France	5.4	5.1	(6%)
Italy	4.6	3.9	(15%)
Canada	3.2	3.4	+6%
Rest of World	50.9	54.0	+6%
World	**100.0**	**100.0**	-

* All credits on current account: Goods + Services + Income + Transfers
Source: *IMF Balance of Payments Statistics Yearbook 2003*, (www.imf.org). The data has not been adjusted for the Rotterdam-Antwerp Effect (Appendix IV) or the Netherlands Distortion (Appendix V).

Table A1.5
Leading Countries' Shares of World Income*

Country	1996 Share %	2002 Share %	Change 2002 v 1996
USA	21.5	20.3	(6%)
Germany	7.8	8.2	+5%
UK	*13.7*	*14.7*	*+7%*
Japan	10.7	7.2	(33%)
France	4.6	6.4	+39%
Italy	3.8	3.4	(11%)
Canada	1.8	1.6	(11%)
Rest of World	36.0	38.2	+6%
World	**100.0**	**100.0**	-

* Income = Earnings on Direct, Portfolio and Lending investments
Source: *IMF Balance of Payments Statistics Yearbook 2003*, (www.imf.org). The data has not been adjusted for the Rotterdam-Antwerp Effect (Appendix IV) or the Netherlands Distortion (Appendix V).

Table A1.6
Leading Countries' Shares of World Earnings on FDI*

Country	1996 Share %	2002 Share %	Change 2002 v 1996
USA	43.1	37.3	(13%)
Germany	5.9	3.9	(34%)
UK	*18.8*	*19.6*	*+4%*
Japan	5.9	4.4	(25%)
France	2.9	5.5	+90%
Italy	0.4	1.6	+300%
Canada	3.3	2.6	(21%)
Rest of World	19.7	25.1	+27%
World	**100.0**	**100.0**	-

* Earnings ('credits') on foreign direct investment
Source: *IMF Balance of Payments Statistics Yearbook 2003*, (www.imf.org). The data has not been adjusted for the Rotterdam-Antwerp Effect (Appendix IV) or the Netherlands Distortion (Appendix V).

Table A1.7
**Percentage Shares of All World Exports
of Merchandise and Commercial Services**

Zone	1993	2002	Increase/(Decrease)
NAFTA*	18.2	17.8	(2%)
Eurozone**	32.8	31.7	(3%)
EU-15†	40.3	39.1	(3%)

* NAFTA: the North American Free Trade Agreement, comprising Canada, the USA and Mexico
** Eurozone: the 12 EU states which have adopted the euro
† EU-15: the Eurozone plus the UK, Denmark and Sweden

Source: *World Trade Organisation: International Trade Statistics 2003*, Tables A4 and A6. Each zone's 'Exports' are the aggregate of the exports of the zone's member states both to each other and to countries outside the zone. www.wto.org

Table A1.8
Percentage Shares of All World Exports of Merchandise

Zone	1993	2002	Increase/(Decrease)
NAFTA*	17.5	17.1	(2%)
Eurozone**	32.3	31.5	(2%)
EU-15†	39.4	37.9	(4%)

* NAFTA: the North American Free Trade Agreement, comprising Canada, the USA and Mexico
** Eurozone: the 12 EU states which have adopted the euro
† EU-15: the Eurozone plus the UK, Denmark and Sweden

Source: *World Trade Organisation: International Trade Statistics 2003*, Tables A4 and A6. Each zone's 'Exports' are the aggregate of the exports of the zone's member states both to each other and to countries outside the zone. www.wto.org

Table A1.9
Percentage Shares of All World Exports of Commercial Services

Zone	1993	2002	Increase/(Decrease)
NAFTA*	20.7	20.5	(1%)
Eurozone**	34.8	32.8	(6%)
EU-15†	43.7	43.7	-

* NAFTA: the North American Free Trade Agreement, comprising Canada, the USA and Mexico
** Eurozone: the 12 EU states which have adopted the euro
† EU-15: the Eurozone plus the UK, Denmark and Sweden
Source: *World Trade Organisation: International Trade Statistics 2003*, Tables A4 and A6. Each zone's 'Exports' are the aggregate of the exports of the zone's member states both to each other and to countries outside the zone. www.wto.org

Table A1.10
Exports of Merchandise only:
Values and Shares: Internal and External EU-15† Exports

Zone	1993 Value $ bn	1993 Share %	2002 Value $bn	2002 Share %	Increase/(Decrease) In Shares
World	3,777	100.0	6,455	100.0	-
External EU Exports	548	14.5	940	14.6	+1%
Internal EU Exports	941	24.9	1,509	23.4	(6%)
Total EU Exports	1,489	39.4	2,449	37.9	(4%)

† EU-15: the Eurozone plus the UK, Denmark and Sweden

Source: *World Trade Organisation: International Trade Statistics 2003*, Tables A4 and A6. Each zone's 'Exports' are the aggregate of the exports of the zone's member states both to each other and to countries outside the zone. www.wto.org

Reliability Rating: AA

Appendix II

Ninety Per Cent or More of the British Economy Is Not Involved in Exports to the EU

The percentage of the economy involved in exporting to EU-14 is calculated by combining government data on exports and on the 'weights' of various sectors of the economy, then adjusting them for distortions to recorded trade flows.

1. All British exports analysed by geographical destination

In 2002, adjusted for two separate distortions, the Rotterdam-Antwerp Effect, relating to Goods and Services, and the Netherlands Distortion, relating to Income (earnings on FDI), the breakdown was as set out in Table A2.1.

Table A2.1
UK Exports: 2002 Real (Post-Adjustment)
Split between EU and Non-EU: £ bn

Category	To EU	To Non-EU	To World	EU/World
Goods + Services*	132	141	**273**	48%
Income†	46	77	**123**	37%
Transfers	8	4	**12**	67%
Total	186	222	**408**	46%

* See Appendix IV: *Distortions To Recorded Trade Flows: The Rotterdam-Antwerp Effect*, esp. Tables 1, 2 and 3
† See Appendix V: *Distortions to Recorded Trade Flows: Foreign Direct Investment: The Netherlands Distortion*

The adjusted share of all UK exports ('credits on current account' in the statistical jargon) worldwide going to the EU varies little from year to year. In 1999, for example, the 'Total' figure was 45 per cent,[1] compared to 46 per cent in 2002. Thus, it seems reasonable to assume that the ratios calculated for 2002 are valid for periods longer than one year.

2. The weight of exports-to-the-EU in the UK economy

The *Supply and Use Tables*[2] published by the ONS base their representation of the 'weights' of various sectors of the economy on the measure 'components of final demand'. 'Final demand' is equivalent to GDP plus imports of goods and services;[3] but it does not capture receipts of income and transfers.

In 2001, according to the Supply and Use Tables, *Exports of Goods and Services Worldwide* accounted for 21 per cent of 'final demand'. From Table A2.1 it can be seen that the adjusted proportion of goods and services going to the EU was 48 per cent. Multiplying 21 per cent by 48 per cent gives ten per cent as the weight of exports-of-goods-and-services-to-the-EU in the UK economy.

Were it possible to include the part of the economy involved in generating 'income' in this measure, it is likely that the overall weight of exports to the EU in the UK economy would drop well below ten per cent, given the much smaller percentage—37 per cent (see Table A2.1)—of income arising in the EU compared to the percentage—48 per cent (see Table A2.1)—in respect of goods and services.

Reliability Rating: A

Appendix III

The World Economy: 1993 to Now

*In 2002, with one per cent of world population, the UK accounted for six per cent (*see Appendix I, p. 55) *of world exports of goods, services, income and transfers, ranking third in the world after the USA and Germany; and for three per cent[1] of world GDP. In the last eleven years the UK has performed quite well, though not as well as many countries outside the EU, while the Eurozone economy under-performed. The structure and pattern of UK trade remains quite different from that of the Eurozone.*

The collapse of Communism in the Soviet Union and Eastern Europe, followed by German reunification, marked a decisive shift in the geo-political assumptions and landscape of the previous 45 years of the Cold War. These events coincided with share price and property 'bubbles' in several advanced economies, followed by recession and—in Europe at least—currency instability. By 1993, recovery had begun. 1993 to 2000 was a period of relative stability, low inflation and sustained economic growth, despite 'hiccups' in a number of Asian and Latin American countries.

The EU's Single Market began operation in 1993 and the introduction of the euro in 1999 was regarded as a technical success. At the end of the decade more 'bubbles' appeared: share prices slumped, though property prices remained high. Most economies faltered in 2001, but following the severe geo-political shock of 9/11, the USA pump-primed its economy, which took off again in 2002. In 2003 US and Chinese growth appeared to be the motor of world growth, pulling in their wake the Japanese and Eurozone economies.

The period 1993-2003 thus covers at least one complete economic cycle, during which the Internet Age arrived, FDI surged and the EU pursued its experiment with economic and political 'integration'. During this period, the UK did quite well, displacing Japan to become the world's third-biggest exporting country and France to become the world's fourth-biggest economy. Meanwhile, the Eurozone economy under-performed, with low growth and high unemployment. Table A3.1 illustrates the contrasting fortunes of selected OECD countries during this period.

Table A3.1
Real GDP Growth: 1993 to 2003
Indexed on 1993=100

Country	Index
Ireland	214
Korea	168
Australia	145
Canada	141
Iceland	139
New Zealand	139
USA	138
Spain	136
Norway	136
UK	*133*
OECD average	130
Netherlands	128
EU-15 average	125
France	123
Eurozone average	*123*
Italy	119
Germany	115
Japan	114
Switzerland	111

Source: Calculated from *OECD Economic Outlook December 2003, Statistical Annex: Table 1*. ww.oecd.org

UK exports (of goods, services, income and transfers) are now proportionately twice as US-oriented as those of Germany and France in particular and of EU-14 in general.[2] Similarly, British exports are proportionately much less EU-oriented than those of the other fourteen EU countries taken together, and of Germany and France in particular.

The UK economy is the least manufacturing-oriented of the seven leading exporting nations (see Appendix I), and correspondingly more services-oriented than many other advanced economies of similar size, partly by virtue of London's role as the world's biggest international financial centre. The UK is the world's second-biggest exporter of commercial services, after the USA, and the biggest in Europe (see Appendix I).

Reliability Rating: A

Appendix IV

Distortions to Recorded Trade Flows:
Trade in Goods and Services:
The Rotterdam-Antwerp Effect

Europe's two biggest ports are Rotterdam, in the Netherlands, and Antwerp, in Belgium. Around two-thirds of British exports of goods and services recorded in the trade statistics[1] as going to and from those countries appear to be transiting via Rotterdam and Antwerp on their way to or from somewhere else, some to end-destinations within other EU countries, the remainder to and from end-destinations outside the EU. Thus, recorded trade with the Netherlands and Belgium, (and with the EU of which they are members) appears to be overstated.

Table A4.1 confirms that, per capita of their populations, the Netherlands and Belgium apparently consume approximately three times as much UK imports of goods and services as do the Germans and French. (Such has been the case for at least the last ten years.)

On the face of it, this seems unlikely. The Netherlands, Belgium, Germany and France have similar GDPs per capita, similar climates and similar lifestyles and all are geographically close neighbours of the UK. The presence in the Netherlands and Belgium of, respectively, the biggest and second-biggest ports in Europe, and the entrepot role of those ports, suggests an explanation for the apparent over-consumption of British imports by those countries.

Table A4.2 shows the effect of assuming that the underlying Dutch and Belgian propensity-to-import-UK-goods-and-services per capita is the same as that of Germany and France, and that two-thirds of UK exports of goods and services to the Netherlands and Belgium transit through those countries on their way somewhere else, half to other EU countries, half outside the EU altogether. Table A4.3 shows the impact of the resulting adjustment on the split of UK goods and services worldwide in 2002 between the EU and countries outside the EU.

64

Table A4.1
UK Recorded Exports of Goods and Services: 2002

£ bn	UK Exports of Goods			
	Exports	Pop. mn†	Exports/Capita £	Index
To Germany	22.02	82.31	268	100
To France	18.72	59.19	316	118
To Netherlands	13.98	15.97	875	326
To Belgium*	10.53	10.67*	987	368
	UK Exports of Services			
To Germany	6.57	82.31	80	100
To France	5.27	59.19	89	111
To Netherlands	4.13	15.97	259	324
To Belgium*	2.39	10.67*	224	280

†   Main Economic Indicators: January 2004, OECD. www.oecd.org
*   Belgian figures include those of Luxembourg, which the ONS does not specify separately

Table A4.2
Adjusting UK Recorded Exports of Goods and Services to the Netherlands and Belgium

£ billion	Assumption			Adjusted 'Real'	
Recorded Exports Goods + Services	⅓ to Netherlands + Belgium*	⅓ to other EU	⅓ to non-EU	To EU-14	To non-EU
31.03	10.35	10.35	10.35	20.68	10.35

*   Belgian figures include those of Luxembourg, which the ONS does not specify separately

Table A4.3
Adjusting UK Recorded Exports of Goods and Services to the World

£ bn	Recorded to EU-14	Recorded to non-EU	Recorded to World	Adjusted 'Real' to EU-14	Adjusted 'Real' to non-EU
Goods and Services	142	131	273	132	141
Percentages	52	48	100	48	52

Reliability Rating: A

Appendix V
Distortions to Recorded Trade Flows: Foreign Direct Investment: The Netherlands Distortion

Because of the Netherlands Distortion, government statistics overstate the importance of the EU as a source of inward investment into the UK, and as a destination for UK outward investment overseas. For tax reasons, FDI is often channelled through intermediate holding companies domiciled in the Netherlands. In such cases government statistics erroneously record that country as the origin of inward investment into the UK and as the end-destination of UK investment overseas.

The real (post-adjustment[1]) geographical pattern of UK FDI flows is set out in the tables.

Table A5.1
Main Inward Investors into the UK

Measured by Earnings AFTER adjustment for the Netherlands distortion

		(%)
By Region	USA + Canada	55
	EU-14	25
	Rest of World	20
		100
By Country	USA	52
	France	9
	Switzerland	4
	Australia + New Zealand	4
	Canada	3
	Germany	3
	Eire	2
	Sweden	2
	Japan*	2
	Belgium/Luxembourg	2

* Note the low position of Japan, often wrongly assumed to be among the most important investors in the UK

Table A5.2
Main Recipients of UK Investment Overseas

Measured by Earnings* AFTER adjustment for the Netherlands distortion

		(%)
By Region	USA + Canada	36
	EU-14	24
	Rest of World	40
		100
By Country	USA	33
	Australia + New Zealand	7
	Eire	4
	France	4
	Belgium/Luxembourg	4
	Germany	4
	Hong Kong	4
	Switzerland	3
	Singapore	3
	Canada	3

*'Earnings': aggregated (cumulative) earnings 1993-2002 inclusive, on all FDI made and received by the UK since records began over a century ago. Source: *Foreign Direct Investment 2002: Business Monitor MA4:* ONS, February 2004. www.statistics.gov.uk

In 2002, the earnings (receipts) on UK foreign direct investment ('FDI') overseas were £52 billion (almost four times the value of UK oil exports, five times the value of UK car exports and 13 per cent of all UK 'credits on current account'). Earnings (payments) to overseas investors in the UK were £17 billion.

At the end of 2002 the net book value of all British FDI overseas was £572 billion, and the net book value of all FDI from overseas in the UK, £353 billion. FDI worldwide, including that involving the UK, grew rapidly in the 1990s, then fell back in 2001 and 2002. The UK is the world's second-biggest outward investor, after the USA, and the third-biggest recipient of FDI, after the USA and 'China-plus-Hong-Kong'. The USA and the UK are each other's principal FDI partners.

Reliability Rating: A

Appendix VI
UK Main Economic Magnitudes

Total UK exports: 2002:   £408 bn

Total UK imports: 2002:   £426 bn

Source: *The Pink Book 2003*, ONS. 'Exports' and 'Imports' consists of trade in goods, services, income and transfers. www.statistics.gov.uk

GDP @ current prices*: £ bn

1999	2000	2001	2002	2003
904	951	994	1,044	1,093

* Source: *The Blue Book 2003*, ONS. www.statistics.gov.uk

Average exchange rates

	2001	2002	2003
£ =	$1.44	$1.50	$1.63
£ =	€1.61	€1.59	€1.45

Source: ECB *Monthly Bulletin*, February 2004. www.ecb.int

Government Expenditure, 2004-2005

	£ bn
Social spending	138
NHS	81
Education	63
Law and Order	29
Defence	27
Debt interest	25
Other personal and social services	22
Industry, agriculture, employment	20
Housing and environment	17
Transport	16
Other expenditure (inc. transfers to EU)	49
Total	**488**

Source: HM Treasury, *Budget Statement*, 17 March 2004, HC 301.
www.hm-treasury.gov.uk

Taxes Raised, 2004-2005

	£ bn
Income tax	128
National insurance	78
VAT	73
Excise duties	40
Corporation tax	35
Council tax	20
Business rates	19
Other*	62
Total	**455**

* includes capital taxes, stamp duties, vehicle excise duties
Source: HM Treasury, *Budget Statement*, 17 March 2004, HC 301.
www.hm-treasury.gov.uk

Reliability rating: AA

Abbreviations and Glossary

Acquis communautaire	The totality of EU legislation and regulation; once power is acquired ('*acquis*' in French) from member states by the EU, it is never given back
BCC	British Chambers of Commerce
'Brussels'	The European Union, and, more generally, the bureaucracy of its institutions: Commission, Parliament, Council, Court of Justice etc.
CAP	The EU Common Agricultural Policy
CET	The EU Common External Tariff
CFP	The EU Common Fisheries Policy
EC	European Community: generally, the pre-1992 name of the European Union; it survives in various EU legal and technical terms
ECB	The Frankfurt-based European Central Bank
ECJ	The Luxembourg-based European Court of Justice
EFTA	European Free Trade Association
EU	The European Union (the name adopted in the Maastricht Treaty of 1992)
EU-15	The 15 member states, including the UK, of the EU prior to the accession of ten new members on 1 May 2004
EU-14	EU-15 less the UK
EU-25	The 25-member EU post 1 May 2004
Eurozone	The 12 member-states that have adopted the euro: EU-15 less the UK, Denmark and Sweden
ERM	The Exchange Rate Mechanism
FDI	Foreign Direct Investment
FTA	Free Trade Agreement
GATT	The General Agreement on Tariffs and Trade, the fore-runner of the WTO
GDP	Gross Domestic Product, a widely-used measure of an economy's size
GSP	The EU Growth and Stability Pact
IFRI	Institut Français des Relations Internationales
IMF	The Washington-based International Monetary Fund
ITC	The (US) International Trade Commission

NAFTA	The North American Free Trade Agreement
NATO	The North Atlantic Treaty Organisation
NIESR	The (British) National Institute for Economic and Social Research
OECD	The Paris-based Organisation for Economic Co-operation and Development
ONS	The (British) Office for National Statistics
PESCO	The Pan-European System of Cumulation of Origin
RIA	Regulatory Impact Assessment
Single (or Internal Market)	The market within the EU Customs Union
VAT	Value Added Tax
WTO	The Geneva-based World Trade Organisation

Notes

Editor's Introduction

1 Figures after enlargement are not yet available.

2 ONS, *The Blue Book 2003*, p. 84. Final demand is calculated by the ONS to remove inconsistencies between the income, expenditure and production methods of calculating GDP.

3 The calculation is 21/100 x 48. If the calculation is based on GDP at market prices, then exports of goods and services make up 26 per cent of the total, which means that exports to the EU account for 12.5 per cent of total national product. ONS, *The Pink Book 2003*, Table 1.2.

4 Pain, N. and Young, G., *Continent Cut Off? The Macroeconomic Impact of British Withdrawal from the EU*, NIESR, February 2000. Republished as 'The macroeconomic impact of UK withdrawal from the EU', *Economic Modelling*, 21 (2004), pp. 387-408. They concluded that there was 'no reason to suppose that unemployment would rise significantly if the UK were to withdraw from the EU'. However, they argued that foreign investment would fall, leading to a reduction in GDP of 2.25 per cent.

5 *The Impact on the US Economy of Including the United Kingdom in a Free Trade Arrangement with the United States, Canada and Mexico*, International Trade Commission, Investigation No. 332-409, Publication No 3339, August 2000. www.usitc.gov

6 ONS, *UK Balance of Payments, The Pink Book 2003*. www.statistics.gov.uk

7 Based on actual tariffs collected and derived from Written Answer P-0472/04EN given in the European Parliament by the Commission (Mrs Schreyer) on 5 March 2004.

8 British Chambers of Commerce, *Burdens Barometer 2004* and *Are regulators raising their game?*, 31 March 2004. www.britishchambers.org.uk

9 Speech by Dutch Vice Prime Minister and Finance Minister, Mr Gerrit Zalm to the UK Government sponsored conference 'Advancing Enterprise: Britain in a Global Economy', 26 January 2004.

10 *OECD Database 1986-2002, Producer and Consumer Support Estimates, Agricultural Policies in OECD Countries: Monitoring and Evaluation*, 2003; its figures are in US dollars. www.oecd.org

11 *UK Balance of Payments, The Pink Book 2003*, Autumn 2003, Table 9.2. www.statistics.gov.uk

12 European Commission, *The Single Market and Tomorrow's Europe: A Progress Report from the European Commission,* 1996; Allen, C., Gasiorek, M., and Smith, A., 'The competition effects of the single market in Europe', *Economic Policy,* 1998, 27, pp. 441-86.

13 *Germany's competitive position and foreign trade within the euro area* (in English): Monthly Report October 2003, Deutsche Bundesbank. www.bundesbank.de

14 Leach, G., *EU Membership: What's the Bottom Line?,* Institute of Directors, March 2000, chapter 6. www.iod.com

15 UK Trade and Investment (formerly Invest UK), *Operations Review* 2003, July 2003. www.invest.uk.com

16 Pain, N., and Young, G., 'The macroeconomic impact of UK withdrawal from the EU', *Economic Modelling,* 21 (2004), pp. 387-408.

17 European Commission, *The EU Economy: 2002 Review,* ELFIN/475/02-EN: 11 December 2002, pp. 197-99.

1: Cost vs Benefit—The Calculus

1 Global Britain Briefing Note No 19, *The Mexico-EU Free Trade Agreement Points the Way,* 1 March 2000.

2 Appendix I: *The World's Seven Biggest Exporting Nations.* HM Government still seems to think that the UK is 'the world's fifth largest trading nation' (*A Constitutional Treaty for the EU – The British Approach to the European Union Intergovernmental Conference 2003,* Cm 5934, September 2003, p. 8).

3 Global Britain Briefing Note No. 30: *European Union 2002 Prosperity Rankings,* 31 October 2003. www.globalbritain.org

2: The Cost of EU Regulation

1 (UK Government) Cabinet Office web-site: www.cabinet-office.gov.uk

2 House of Lords, 13 January 2003, Written Answer by Baroness Symons to a Question (HL 649) from Lord Stoddart, WA 13, Hansard.

3 British Chambers of Commerce: *Burdens Barometer 2004* and *Are regulators raising their game?,* 31 March 2004; www.britishchambers.org.uk

4 A letter from the House of Commons Library dated 5 May 2004 to Stephen O'Brien MP, identifying the BCC Burdens Barometer's legislative acts originating in the EU, allows the exact percentage by value to be put at 83 per cent.

5   Speech to the UK government sponsored conference, 'Advancing Enterprise: Britain in a Global Economy', 26 January 2004.

6   Institute of Directors: www.iod.com

3: The Common Agricultural Policy (CAP)

1   Mr Blair, speech in The Hague, 20 January 1998.

2   Mr Brown, speech in Bournemouth, 29 September 2003.

3   Global Britain Briefing Note No. 30, *EU 2002 Prosperity Rankings*, 31 October 2003: www.globalbritain.org

4   The European Commission, *The 2003 Agricultural Year*, www.europa.eu.int/comm

5   Box 5.3, Budget *Red Book*, 17 March 2004, HC 301, HM Treasury; its CAP figures are in US dollars. www.hm-treasury.gov.uk

6   *OECD Database 1986-2002, Producer and Consumer Support Estimates, Agricultural Policies in OECD Countries: Monitoring and Evaluation: 2003*; its figures are in US dollars. www.oecd.org

7   Global Britain Briefing Note No. 30, *EU 2002 Prosperity Rankings*, 31 October 2003. www.globalbritain.org

8   See Hindley, B. and Howe, M., *Better Off Out?,* Institute of Economic Affairs, 2001, Appendix A, for a discussion of the costs of CAP, including OECD underestimation of costs. www.iea.org

9   See Table C 11, Budget *Red Book*, 17 March 2004, HC 301, p. 266.

10   The European Commission, *The 2003 Agricultural Year.* www.europa.eu.int/comm

11   WTO *Annual Report 2003*, April 2003, p. 22: '...the EU [..] accounts for 90% of export subsidies granted by OECD countries...'. www.wto.org

4: The EU Budget

1   Three recent government publications give three different figures for the 2002 'net contribution'. HM Treasury's Budget Statement of 17 March 2004 gives (p. 266) £2.3 billion (admittedly for the 2002/03 fiscal year). The ONS *Blue Book* of autumn 2003 gives £3.0 billion for calendar year 2002. HM Treasury's *European Community Finances: Statement on the 2003 EC Budget (*see below) gives £3.6 billion for calendar year 2002. The Commission, which works on a calendar year basis, gives a different figure again. The Treasury document referenced below, which comes out once a year, has a stab at reconciling the differences.

2   *European Community Finances: Statement on the 2003 EC Budget,* HM Treasury, Cm 5800, April 2003. www.hm-treasury.gov.uk

3   *UK Balance of Payments: The Pink Book 2003*: *Table 9.2*; ONS, autumn 2003. www.statistics.gov.uk

4   'Many commentators focus on the net figure when estimating the direct costs of membership. However, this is misleading. When estimating the domestic tax burden we do not deduct public expenditure from the total tax burden. We don't say income tax is zero because of spending on health and education. Consistency demands that we adopt the same policy towards payments—which are essentially a tax—to the EU'. Leach, G., *EU Membership: What's the Bottom Line?*, Institute of Directors, March 2000. www.iod.com

5: The Single Market

1   See for example 'Benefits of the European Union', in *A Constitutional Treaty for the European Union: the British Approach to the EU Intergovernmental Conference 2003*, Cm 5934, Foreign and Commonwealth Office, September 2003. www.fco.gov.uk

2   *Germany's competitive position and foreign trade within the euro area* (in English): Monthly Report, Deutsche Bundesbank, October 2003. www.bundesbank.de

3   Leach, G., *EU Membership: What's the Bottom Line?* Institute of Directors, March 2000, chapter 6: *The EU–external and internal trade liberalisation.* www.iod.com

4   *Germany's competitive position and foreign trade within the euro area* (in English): Monthly Report, Deutsche Bundesbank, October 2003. www.bundesbank.de; Global Britain Briefing Notes, No. 29: *French Exports after the Euro,* 31 October 2003; No. 28: *German Exports after the Euro,* 3 October 2003; No. 27: *Single Market: USA Main Beneficiary,* 6 June 2003; No. 25: *World Exports: Winners and Losers,* 21 February 2003; www.globalbritain.org. See also Robin, J-P., 'Pourquoi la France perd autant de parts de marché', *Figaro Economie,* 25 March 2004; Rodier, A., 'La France perd du terrain en Asie', *Figaro Economie,* 2 April 2004; Appendix I: *The World's Seven Biggest Exporting Nations;* Appendix III: *The World Economy: 1993 to now.*

5   Global Britain Briefing Note No. 30: *European Union 2002 Prosperity Rankings*, 31 October 2003. ww.globalbritain.org

6: The Importance of Inward Investment to the UK Economy

1   *World Investment Report 2003*, UNCTAD, July 2003, Annex Tables B5 and B6. www.unctad.org

2   *World Invisible Trade 2003*, International Financial Services, (formerly 'British Invisibles'), November 2003, p. 5; *World Investment Report 2003*, 2003, Annex Tables B5 and B7. www.ifsl.org.uk

3   *Invest UK Annual Review 2003*, July 2003. www.invest.uk.com

4   Global Britain Briefing Note No. 7, *Inward investment: the irrelevance of the Single Market*, 17 March 2000. www.globalbritain.org

5   Harris and Robinson, *The unpredictable impact of FDI on domestic productivity in the UK: Productivity Impacts and Spillovers from Foreign Ownership in the UK*, National Institute Economic Review No. 187, January 2004. www.niesr.ac.uk

7: Opportunity Cost

1   Prime Minister, speech in The Hague, 20 January 1998.

8: Future Costs and Benefits of EU Membership

1   For example, Keith Vaz, then Minister for 'Europe', who said of the Charter *'that it had no more importance than the Beano'*.

2   'New EU constitution would lead to more red tape and make economic reform less likely', Letter from Geoffrey Fitchew, *Financial Times*, 11 May 2004.

3   'Enlargement could add £1.75 bn to UK GDP', *A Constitutional Treaty for the EU: The British Approach to the European Union Intergovernmental Conference 2003*, Cm 5934, FCO, September 2004, p. 15. www.fco.gov.uk £1.75 billion is about one six-hundredth of UK GDP!

4   'Enlargement could add £1.75 bn to UK GDP', *A Constitutional Treaty for the EU: The British Approach to the European Union Intergovernmental Conference 2003*, Cm 5934, 2004.

5   *Germany's competitive position and foreign trade within the euro area* (in English): Monthly Report, Deutsche Bundesbank, October 2003. www bundesbank.de

6   Debate, *EU Taxation* (esp. speech by Baroness Noakes), House of Lords, 25 February 2004, Hansard Cols 313-327; Debate, *EU Constitutional Treaty*, House of Lords, 11May 2004, Hansard Cols 173-244. www.parliament.the-stationery-office.co.uk

7   Leach, G., *EU Membership: What's the Bottom?*, Institute of Directors, March 2000. www.iod.com

8   Global Britain Briefing Notes Nos 18, *Demographic Change, 2000-2050*, and 26, *Old Europe, Young America*. (www.globalbritain.org). See also *Living Happily Ever After: The Economic Implications of Aging Societies: Standards of Living in Mature Economies Jeopardised by Impact of Aging;* World Economic Forum, January 2004. www.weforum.org

9   Title II, Article 103 of the (post-Nice) Consolidated Treaty establishing the European Community.

10 ECB *Monthly Bulletin,* March 2004. www.ecb.int

11 *'It's quite striking that when I'm with Tony Blair and Gerhard Schröder I'm more or less the furthest to the left'*, Jean-Pierre Raffarin, Prime Minister of a French 'right-wing' government, interview in *Le Monde*, 17 January 2004.

12 Part One, Title 1, Article 1-3.3: *The Union's Objectives; The Draft Treaty Establishing a Constitution for Europe,* text and commentary published by British Management Data Foundation as of 5 September 2003. www.bmdf.co.uk and www.eurotreaties.com

9: Recent Cost-Benefit Analyses

1   Pain, N. and Young, G., *Continent Cut Off? The Macroeconomic Impact of British Withdrawal from the EU*, NIESR, February 2000. Republished as 'The macroeconomic impact of UK withdrawal from the EU', *Economic Modelling*, 21 (2004), pp. 387-408. They conclude that there was 'no reason to suppose that unemployment would rise significantly if the UK were to withdraw from the EU'. However, they argued that foreign investment would fall leading to a reduction in GDP of 2.25 per cent.

2   Leach, G., *EU Membership: What's the Bottom Line?*, Institute of Directors, March 2000. www.iod.com

3   *The Impact on the US Economy of Including the United Kingdom in a Free Trade Arrangement with the United States, Canada and Mexico, International Trade Commission*, Investigation No. 332-409, Publication No. 3339, August 2000. www.usitc.gov

4   Hindley, B. and Howe, M., *Better Off Out?*, Institute of Economic Affairs, 2001. www.iea.org.uk

5   President Chirac, addressing the entire Paris-based Diplomatic Corps on 8 January 2004, announced that 'in spring, France will present to her partners the conclusions on new sources of international financing, in particular the taxation of financial exchanges [he meant the so-called Tobin Tax] issued by the multi-disciplinary working group I have brought together. ...' No prizes for guessing which of France's 'partners' would be hardest hit by

such a tax. On 7 April 2004, in 'L'Europe de la mondialisation maîtrisée', in *Figaro*, Pascal Lamy, the Commissioner for Trade, called for an EU corporation tax to do away with differing national systems of taxing business.

6   Quoted in Leach, *EU Membership: What's the Bottom Line?*, 2000.

7   Minford, P., *The Economic Consequences of EU Membership: a Stock-taking*, Liverpool Macroeconomic Research Quarterly Economic Bulletin, Vol. 24, No. 3, September 2003.

8   Unpublished. Discussed by John Murray and the author in 1995.

9   Miller, M.H., *Estimates of the Static Balance of Payments and Welfare Costs of UK Entry into the Common Market*, National Institute Economic Review, No. 57, August 1971.

10: The UK in the World Trading System

1   For a comprehensive discussion of the world trading system, including its organisation, **structures** and mechanisms, the differences between FTAs and customs unions, EFTA, PESCOs, the Swiss example etc, see the following Global Britain Briefing Notes: Nos 5, 8, 11, 15 (all four by Ronald Stewart-Brown), 19, 25, 27, 28, 29, 30 and 31 (www.globalbritain.org); see also Walsh, J., *EU Enlargement: not all it's cracked up to be*, IoD, June 2003. www.iod.com

2   *UK Balance of Payments: The Pink Book 2003*, ONS, autumn 2003. www.statistics.gov.uk

3   *World Trade Report 2003*, WTO, ISBN 92-870-1230, 2003. www.wto.org

4   For a comprehensive discussion of the world trading system, including its organisation, structures and mechanisms, the differences between FTAs and customs unions, EFTA, PESCOs, the Swiss example etc, see the following Global Britain Briefing Notes: Nos 5, 8, 11, 15 (all four by Ronald Stewart-Brown), 19, 25, 27, 28, 29, 30 and 31 (www.globalbritain.org); see also Walsh, *EU Enlargement: not all it's cracked up to be*, 2003. www.iod.com

5   EFTA: European Free Trade Association, headquartered in Geneva, comprising Iceland, Lichtenstein, Norway and Switzerland. Having been a founder-member, the UK left EFTA in 1973 to join the then EC.

6   US-Australia FTA, 1 March 2004, Office of the United States Trade Representative. www.ustr.gov

7   Global Britain Briefing Note No. 19, *The Mexico-EU Free Trade Agreement Points the Way*, 1 March 2000. www.globalbritain.org

8   Stewart-Brown, R., Global Britain Briefing Note No. 5, *The World Trade Organisation*, 19 November 1999.

9   *2004 Index of Economic Freedom*, The Heritage Foundation/*The Wall Street Journal*, 2004. www.heritage.org

10 Percentages derived from Written Answer P-0472/04EN given in the European Parliament by the Commission (Mrs Schreyer) on 5 March 2004.

11 Stewart-Brown, R., Global Britain Briefing Note No. 5, *The World Trade Organisation*, 19 November 1999.

12 Written Answer (HL1589) to Written Question, House of Lords, 11 March 2004. www.parliament.the-stationery-office.co.uk

13 Written Answer (HL 1591) to Written Question, House of Lords, 11 March 2004.

14 Written Answer (HL 1590) to Written Question, House of Lords, 11 March 2004.

15 *UK Balance of Payments: The Pink Book 2003*, ONS, 2003, Table 9.4. www.statistics.gov.uk

16 *UK Balance of Payments: The Pink Book 2003*, ONS, 2003, Table 9.4. www.statistics.gov.uk

17 *Annual Abstract of Statistics 2004*, ONS, 2004, Table 19.4. www.statistics.gov.uk

18 *UK Balance of Payments: The Pink Book 2003*, ONS, 2003, Table 9.4. www.statistics.gov.uk

19 Written Answer (HL 1893) to Written Question, House of Lords, 24 March 2004.

20 Written Answer (HL 1592) to Written Question, House of Lords, 11 March 2004.

21 *UK Balance of Payments: The Pink Book 2003*, ONS, 2003, Table 9.4. www.statistics.gov.uk

11: The Coming Decline of the EU?

1   Global Britain Briefing Note No. 18, *Demographic Change 2000-2050*, 15 February 2002, and No. 26, *Old Europe, Young America*, 25 April 2003. www.globalbritain.org

2   Global Britain Briefing Note No. 18, *Demographic Change 2000-2050*, 15 February 2002, and No. 26, *Old Europe, Young America*, 25 April 2003. www.globalbritain.org

3   *Living Happily Ever After: the Economic Implications of Ageing Societies*, World Economic Forum/Watson Wyatt Worldwide, 19 January 2004, www.weforum.org

4   Joint letter from Messrs Blair, Chirac and Schröder to Messrs Ahern and Prodi, 18 February 2004; '... *Europe is currently faced with a demographic slowdown and an ageing population. This situation is troubling and calls for an urgent response ... in the context of demographic slowdown, growth and productivity in Europe remain too weak ...*'

5   Mr Gerrit Zalm, speech, 26 January 2004: '... because of the ageing of Europe, governments are confronted with a huge challenge to guarantee sustainable public finances...'

6   Dr Denis McShane MP, Minister for Europe, interview in *Figaro Magazine*, 26 April 2003, '... *today the European [EU-15] economy produces 20 per cent less than the US economy ... according to economists at the Foreign Office, by 2010 the European economy will produce 40 per cent less than the US economy ...*'

7   Annex B para. 9, *The exchange rate and macroeconomic adjustment* (one of the supporting studies issued on 9 June 2003 as part of the *Assessment of the Five Economic Tests)*, HM Treasury: '*There are good (sic!) reasons to think that the relative importance of the euro bloc will decline over time. Developing economies tend to grow faster than developed economies, and most are in the US dollar bloc. In addition ... potential growth in the US itself is still thought to be higher than in Europe.*' www.hm-treasury.gov.uk

8   In evidence to the House of Commons Treasury Committee, *The UK and the Euro*, Sixth Report of Session 2002-03, Vol II: Minutes of Evidence and Appendices, HoC 187-II, ISBN 0 215 01054 X, The Stationery Office, 7 May 2003. www.parliament.uk

9   Ferguson, N., *The End of Europe ?*, Bradley Lecture, American Enterprise Institute, 4 March 2004. www.aei.org

10 Baverez, N., *La France Qui Tombe*, Perrin, August 2003, ISBN 2-262-021201; Fitoussi, J-P., (a strong supporter of the 'European Project') *La Règle et le Choix*, Editions du Seuil et La République des Idées, September 2002, ISBN 2-02-055674-5; Cotta, A., *Une Glorieuse Stagnation*, Fayard, April 2003, ISBN 2-213-61205-6.

11 Kagan, R., *Paradise and Power: America and Europe in the New World Order*, Atlantic Books, 2003, ISBN 1-84354-177-7.

12 Global Britain Briefing Note No. 26, *Old Europe, Young America*, 25 April 2003. www.globalbritain.org

13 Colombani, P., *Le Commerce Mondial au 21e siècle: Scénarios pour L'Union Européenne*, Institut Français des Relations Internationales, November 2002. www.ifri.org

14 Wilson, D., *Dreaming With BRICS: The Path to 2050*; Global Economics Paper No. 99, Goldman Sachs, October 2003. www.gs.com

Appendix II

1 See Global Britain Briefing Note No. 22, *Ninety per cent of the British economy is NOT involved in Exports to the EU*, 20 September 2002.

2 Table 2.1: *Supply and Use Tables for the United Kingdom*, in *United Kingdom National Accounts: The Blue Book 2003*, ONS. 2001 is the latest year for which Supply and Use data is given. www.statistics.gov.uk

3 See the Briefing Note No. 22 at ref. 1 above for a more detailed discussion of the different ways of measuring the size of the economy.

Appendix III

1 *World Economic Outlook*, IMF, September 2003.

2 Global Britain Briefing Note No. 27, *Single Market: USA Main Beneficiary*, 6 June 2003.

Appendix IV

1 *United Kingdom Balance of Payments: The Pink Book 2003*, ONS, October 2003. www.statistics.gov.uk

Appendix V

1 The adjustment assumes that the 'real' level of Dutch FDI in the UK, and of UK FDI in the Netherlands, is the same per capita of the Dutch population as the recorded levels of inward and outward EU-13 (that is, EU-14 less the Netherlands). See Global Britain Briefing Note No. 32, *Foreign Direct Investment: The Netherlands Distortion: 2004 Update*, 4 June 2004, for the detailed calculations. www.globalbritain.org